The Ex-Offender's Job Interview Guide

Turn Your *Red Flags* Into *Green Lights*

Second Edition

Ronald L. Krannich, Ph.D.

IMPACT PUBLICATIONS
Manassas, Virginia

Publisher: For information on Impact Publications, including current and forthcoming publications, authors, press kits, online bookstore, newsletters, downloadable catalogs, and submission requirements, visit www.impactpublications.com.

Publicity/Rights: For information on publicity, author interviews, and subsidiary rights, contact the Media Relations Department: Tel. 703-361-7300, Fax 703-335-9486, or email: query@impactpublications.com.

Sales/Distribution: All special sales and distribution inquiries should be directed to the publisher: Sales Department, IMPACT PUBLICATIONS, 7820 Sudley Road, Suite 100, Manassas, VA 20109, Tel. 703-361-7300, 912-777-4878, Fax 703-335-9486, or email: query@impactpublications.com. All bookstores sales are handled through Impact's trade distributor: National Book Network, 15200 NBN Way, Blue Ridge Summit, PA 17214, Tel. 1-800-462-6420.

Quantity Discounts: We offer quantity discounts on bulk purchases. Please review our discount schedule for this book at www.impactpublications.com or contact the Special Sales Department, Tel. 703-361-7300.

The Author: Ronald L. Krannich, Ph.D., is one of today's leading career and travel writers who has authored more than 100 books, including several self-help guides for people in transition and those with not-so-hot backgrounds. A former Peace Corps Volunteer, Fulbright Scholar, university professor, and management trainer, Ron specializes in producing and distributing books, DVDs, training programs, and related materials on employment, career transition, addiction, anger management, criminal justice, life skills, and travel. He can be contacted at ron@impactpublications.com. The first edition of this book (2009) was co-authored with Ron's deceased wife, Caryl Rae Krannich, Ph.D. On August 4, 2008, the day after completing this book and a companion re-entry book, *The Ex-Offender's Re-Entry Success Guide*, Caryl passed away suddenly. She lived a very good life and one on purpose. This book represents one of her many legacies. She has been sorely missed by many who loved her dearly and who continue to celebrate her all-too-short but very meaningful life.

Contents

1

Speaking Truth to Power

"Tell me about yourself."
"There's a time gap on your resume. Can you explain?"
"Have you ever been convicted of a crime?"

EX-OFFENDERS MUST DO very well in the job interview to get a **job offer**. Knowing the **odds** may be stacked against them and that **rejections** are all part of the job search game, they must go that extra mile with **preparation, preparation, and preparation** to ace the interview.

That's what this book is all about – quickly getting you up and running with great preparation to ace job interviews and get job offers despite red flags in your background. It's all about speaking **truth** to power in a way that makes you especially attractive to employers looking to hire people who will bring **value** to their operations. No lies, no tricks – just the truth focused on **employers' needs**.

Surviving and Succeeding

If you are reading this book, it's a pretty sure bet that either you or someone you care about is soon getting out of prison or already has been released from prison. Perhaps this has happened recently or maybe it has been a while. In any case, you or that person are joining the free world where few things are actually free, a reality you'll immediately face when securing your documentation and looking for housing, food, transportation, and a job. Unfortunately, for many ex-offenders, this whole re-entry process is a struggle for survival against some not-so-good odds of succeeding on the outside. But the odds get much better if you can land a good job, which first and foremost requires excellent job interview skills.

Re-Entry and Jobs

There are a lot of things a person has to deal with as he or she re-enters society and makes the necessary adjustments to living in a community outside the prison walls.

Some feelings are positive, such as it's good to put the bars behind and be back on the outside.

But while freedom can be euphoric, it also brings new **responsibilities** to the ex-offender. How will I be re-integrated with my family? Or if the family ties are weak or non-existent, the anxieties are more related to basic survival. Where will I live? How will I feed myself? At the heart of survival questions about food and shelter is this question: *"How am I going to support myself?"* For most people, the answer relates to employment: *"I need to find a job."* And in order to find the job, you need to do well at the job interview where you will come face-to-face with reluctant employers who have conducted background checks of your history.

Having a job is a critical element determining how well an ex-offender is integrated back into the community. Having a job is one of the best predictors of whether an ex-offender stays out of trouble or whether he commits another crime and re-enters the prison system. Having a job provides both a means of monetary support for the essentials of life and positive feelings of self-worth. Having a really good job means the possibility of also having a long-term career.

Carrying Negative Baggage

But being an ex-offender with a criminal record brings a lot of negative baggage. By law, ex-offenders are prohibited from employment in certain jobs, and many employers are hesitant to hire an ex-offender for any job. But before you let this reality of 'life after incarceration' make you feel the situation is hopeless, consider these statistics about offenders in the United States:

- Over 650,000 ex-offenders are released into communities each year.
- Over 12 million people circulate in and out of prisons, jails, and detention centers each year.
- Over 2.3 million people are currently incarcerated.
- Over 5 million people are on parole or probation.
- Over 77 million people have an arrest record.

Ex-offenders often end up with a self-fulfilling prophecy – low-paying, dead-end jobs no one else wants.

There are a lot of ex-offenders out there, and ex-offenders are hired for jobs every day. So why can't you be one of them? It will take some extra effort on your part. You will need to be better prepared than the person who doesn't have a criminal record to overcome objections (sometimes voiced, but often not mentioned) about your criminal past. But with some hard work in preparation for interviews (as well as other aspects of the job search) you ought to be able to join the thousands of ex-offenders who are gainfully employed.

Key Job Search Mistakes Ex-Offenders Make

Let's address up-front one of the more important mistakes ex-offenders make: they look for "ex-offender jobs" or "ex-offender-friendly employers" who are known to often hire ex-offenders. By limiting their focus in this manner, they create a self-fulfilling prophecy – they are attracted to low paying, high turnover, hard labor, and dead end jobs no one else wants. Indeed, it's not surprising to find ex-offenders disproportionately working as roofers, landscapers, movers, sanitation workers, and day laborers on construction projects. Instead, ex-offenders should be looking for employers who want to hire individuals with their particular skills and then clearly communicate their skills and other important qualities to those employers by way of resumes, applications, and interviews. By doing this, they open themselves to a whole different world of jobs that have promising futures. I outline many of these promising jobs in ***Best Jobs for Ex-Offenders: 101 Opportunities to Jump-Start Your New Life*** (Impact Publications, 2016). Your first job out should be a good stepping stone to more promising jobs and careers – not one that will continue to keep you down.

Ask the Right Questions, Focus on What's Important

Believe it or not, I often hear from ex-offenders who ask me this somewhat puzzling question for specific states and cities:

Do you have a list of employers who hire ex-offenders?

A few ex-offenders even think someone must publish state-by-state and city-by-city directories of "Employers Who Hire Ex-Offenders"! It's a question that tells me volumes about why these inquisitive ex-offenders are going to have trouble finding and keeping a job. Simply put, they don't understand employers and the job market, nor do they have a clue about what they need to do in order to find a good job. If they did, they would consult my other directory *(The Ex-Offender's Re-Entry Assistance Directory*, Impact Publications, 2016) as well as ask a very different type of question:

Who's most interested in my skills?

This question assumes the individual knows what it is he or she does well and enjoys doing – the very foundation of conducting an effective job search with employers who are in the business of hiring talented individuals rather than finding a place of employment for ex-offenders. Remember, employers are not social experiments on trying out ex-offenders in their workplace. They need smart people who can do specific jobs. In other words, they **hire specific skills sets** – not people with difficult backgrounds. If you are only prepared to talk about your criminal background, no one will want to hire you. Indeed, you've got to get smart and **talk about what's really important** – what you are prepared to do for the employer in terms of your workplace skills and behavior. What **value** do you bring to the workplace? Do you come to work **on time**? Are you a **hard worker** who stays **focused** on doing a good job? Are you **accurate?** Are you a **problem-solver**? Do you take **initiative** or do you have to be closely supervised and told what to do? Are you a team player who **gets along** with everyone? Can you **communicate** well with customers and fellow workers? That's the type of skills employers want to hire rather than adopt an ex-offender in need of a job.

So what do you have to offer employers in exchange for their paycheck? What stories are you prepared to tell employers about yourself in reference to their needs?

You're Risky Business for Employers

Ex-offenders are risky business for many employers who prefer hiring people with clean records. Even though you have done your sentence time, you can't really hide your past for long in today's high-tech and social media environment. In many respects, you received **two sentences** when you were convicted – one you already served in prison or jail and the other that you'll serve for the rest of your life as an ex-con with a record. If you were convicted of a felony, you may, for example, face legal restrictions on the types of jobs you can hold, and you may be prohibited from traveling abroad. Many ex-offenders find their life sentence to be a major barrier to success in the free world. Since their records can be easily and inexpensively accessed by employers, they have nowhere to hide in the so-called free world that is not particularly ex-offender-friendly!

Always keep in mind that employers are not social workers who are in the business of giving people a second, third, or fourth chance. So don't beg, lie, manipulate, or try to game the system. Put yourself in their shoes and focus on what's really important to them. After all, they have a bottom line that needs to be maintained and expanded by employing individuals who have the motivation and talent to get things done. They want to **hire talented individuals** – not risky ex-offenders who don't know what they want to do.

Consider the Employer's Needs

Put yourself in the shoes of an employer who may consider interviewing and hiring an ex-offender. He or she is likely to ask the following questions:

- *Why should I hire you?*
- *Will your background pose problems for others you work with?*
- *Are you a trustworthy, responsible, and predictable person?*
- *Do you do what you say and say what you do?*
- *Have you made the necessary changes to become a productive employee?*

Above all, employers want to hire individuals who are a good "fit" for the organization – those who have the right attitudes and behaviors to become productive employees. They do this by trying to understand your **pattern of behavior** during job interviews.

Focus on the Job Interview

This book is all about better preparing you for the critical job interview. In fact, it may well become the most important book you read as part of your re-entry preparation.

It shows you how to turn a job interview into a job offer – one of the most important transitions you need to quickly experience in the free world.

Few people are hired for jobs without going through an interview. An interview is one of the most important steps an applicant goes through in the process of getting a job. It can also be the most nerve-racking because you are meeting the interviewer face to face. It's hard to hide your nervousness – your uncertainty. Everything you say and do is making an impression, either good or bad, on the employer. In fact, even what you do not say may be noticed, and that too may work to your advantage or disadvantage. So it is important that you get the interview right! Spend enough time preparing for the interview, with the help of this book, so that you put your best foot forward and make the very best impression you possibly can. Much of your future depends on it.

Transform Your Life With a Good Job

I wish you well as you take the next important steps toward re-entry into the free world. While you will eventually find a job, even many jobs, raise your bar by trying to land a good job with a promising future. Such a job may well transform your life as you leave the bars behind for good!

2

Red Flags in Your Past

"People with red flags in their background need to turn obvious negatives into positives – convert those red flags into green lights!

ANYONE LOOKING FOR A JOB should anticipate encountering questions about his or her background. But you'll have additional obstacles to overcome if there is something in your past that raises a red flag in the interviewer's mind. Many of the red flags may not have anything to do with whether you are an ex-offender, but they can complicate your job search. Do you have little or no work experience? Have you been a job hopper? That is, do you have a past that is filled with lots of jobs but with a short amount of time spent working at each one? Do you lack a high school diploma or a GED? Have you ever been fired from a job? And, finally, have you ever been convicted of a crime?

Job Knockouts

Red flags can become knockouts to getting job offers since red flags indicate a history of behaviors on the part of the job applicant that may pose problems on the job. Problems with employees are something that employers would prefer to avoid. If you will soon be released from prison or if you have been released, whether recently or some time ago, you are aware that a prison record is just that – a record that stays with you. As a life sentence, **your record** is a very big red flag to a potential employer.

Employers are looking both for positive reasons to hire you and negative reasons not to hire you. They look for positive signs that tell them you are the right person for the job. At the same time, they are searching for clues that tell them not to hire you – that you are going to create more problems than you will solve. Being naturally suspicious of applicants who may be putting on a positive face to get the job offer, they are especially sensitive to any negative signs (red flags) that tell them you may be a potential problem employee. Whatever the red flags from your past, you need to know how to deal with them in an honest, yet positive way.

Remember that red flags relate to **behaviors**. While having been in prison is a red flag in itself, it is what you did to get convicted and sent to prison – the behavior(s) – that is the employer's real concern. But before we go any further with a discussion of red flag behaviors, you need to take stock of your situation. You can't deal with overcoming your personal red flags until you know what your red flag behaviors are and how they may be interpreted by employers.

Test Your Knockout Potential

Respond to the following statements to identify how many red flags you have in your background. Circle the numbers to the right of each statement that best represents your degree of agreement or disagreement:

1 = Strongly disagree   4 = Agree
2 = Disagree   5 = Strongly agree
3 = Maybe, not certain

1. I have no work experience at all.   1 2 3 4 5

2. I have work experience, but very different work from what I want to do in the future.   1 2 3 4 5

3. My grades in school were not very good.   1 2 3 4 5

4. I have no high school diploma or GED.   1 2 3 4 5

5. I have been fired from one job.   1 2 3 4 5

6. I have been fired from more than one job.   1 2 3 4 5

7. I have not stayed at any job for very long.   1 2 3 4 5

8. The jobs I have held have been very different from each other in terms of the work to be done and skills required.   1 2 3 4 5

9. I don't have a past employer who would give me a good reference.   1 2 3 4 5

10. I have been convicted of a felony.   1 2 3 4 5

TOTAL _____

If you circled a "1" or "2" for any of the above statements, your background may raise a red flag in the eyes of most employers. If your total score is between 10 and 35, you will also most likely appear to have a not-so-hot background in the eyes of most employers. You will need to develop interview strategies to overcome the objections and fears you will raise in most interviewers. I'll help you do this in a later section.

Why Do Employers Care About My Past?

Employers care about your past, because they want to hire employees who have the background to do the job. Yes, they want to know about the knowledge you have learned and skills you have developed. But they are just as interested in how dependable you have been – especially attendance, being on time, and ability to stick to a job until the task is completed. These are issues relating to your **character**. They want more than just verbal confirmation that you are a good worker who can be trusted to perform well on the job.

Employers tell us that the following qualities are especially important when they are making a hiring decision.

- They look at an applicant's educational background and past work experience to give them an indication of what they can expect from the person in the future. Completing high school or earning a GED is evidence not only an applicant's having achieved a level of basic competence, but it's also an indicator of their motivation to finish a task and achieve goals. The higher an individual's educational achievement, the more likely he or she possesses an important character trait that transfers to the workplace – **persistence**.

- Work experience also is an indicator of what the individual has done in the past and is likely to do in the future – both in terms of how well the job was done and how **dependable** the applicant was as an employee. Could the previous employer(s) depend on the individual to be at work, be there on time, and stay focused on getting the job done?

- In the case of ex-offenders, employers are most impressed with recommendations provided by former employers who actually worked with the ex-offender rather than relatives, prison personnel, or faith-based workers who frequently give ex-offenders a soft pass on recommendations (bless their good hearts, but they are often motivated to see their clients succeed rather than provide candid insights into their positives and negatives). Do you have a previous employer(s) who will give you a good recommendation? References from former employers, especially one from a supervisor in a recent work release program, carry more weight than personal references when an employer is making a hiring decision.

- Employers prefer hiring ex-offenders with transitional work experience rather than those who only completed an educational and training program while in prison or have work experience prior to their conviction. Transitional work experience, such as participation in a work release program, gives employers direct evidence of recent workplace skills and accomplishments. It tells them a great deal about an individual's current attitudes and workplace behavior.

Employers prefer hiring ex-offenders with transitional work experience.

- Employers tend to hire ex-offenders for positions that involve little direct customer contact – manufacturing, construction, and various outdoor jobs involving little human contact. Therefore, if you apply for a job involving a great deal of customer contact, your red flags may be magnified.

- Once hired, did the applicant stay with each job for a reasonably lengthy period of time? After all, it is time consuming and expensive to hire a new employee. For most jobs it takes several weeks or more before the new hire is truly earning his paycheck. Someone who has had several jobs but stayed in each one only for a few weeks or months is likely to repeat the pattern and leave the next job after a short period of time. Job hoppers are not in great demand by employers.

- And the final red flag: does the applicant have a criminal record? This often appears on the job application as, *"Have you been convicted of a felony?"* While hundreds of states, counties, and cities now prohibit the inclusion of this discriminatory question on applications as part of the "ban the box" movement, nonetheless, you may still encounter it in some places when you complete an application. It is a legitimate question to ask at the job interview. The reason for concern on the part of the employer is the assumed pattern of behavior. If you committed a crime in the past, it is assumed you are more likely to commit one in the future than the applicant who does not have a criminal record. It is easier for the employer to avoid the potential problem by hiring the individual without the criminal past. Unfair? Perhaps. After all, you have done your time. But to argue the fairness will not get you the job. To ignore reality will not get you the job. You must know that, whether spoken or not, this concern will weigh heavily in the hiring decision. So you must deal with overcoming the employer's concerns – whether spoken or unspoken. The good news it that you will not be screened out of a job interview where it's now illegal to ask this question. At least you will have a chance to get the interview where you must then be prepared to answer the question a face-to-face. This book will help you deal with this issue in the job interview.

Red Flag Behaviors

List your red flag behaviors, including, but not limited to, those behaviors that resulted in your conviction. Include any red flag behaviors from jobs you have held – within or outside of prison. For each behavior, indicate why it might concern a potential employer.

Red Flag Behaviors	**Reasons for Concern to Employer** (*How does the employer think this behavior might affect my future work?*)
1. _____	_____
_____	_____
_____	_____
2. _____	_____
_____	_____
_____	_____

3. _____   _____
   _____   _____
   _____   _____

4. _____   _____
   _____   _____
   _____   _____

5. _____   _____
   _____   _____
   _____   _____

6. _____   _____
   _____   _____
   _____   _____

7. _____   _____
   _____   _____
   _____   _____

8. _____   _____
   _____   _____
   _____   _____

9. _____   _____
   _____   _____
   _____   _____

10. _____   _____
    _____   _____
    _____   _____

Maybe you listed ten red flags and could have listed even more. Maybe you listed fewer than ten. Perhaps you were easily able to list behaviors that you suspected would cause you future employability problems. Let's put this list of red flag behaviors you have just completed aside for the moment. We'll come back to it later. For now, let's try to look at employment issues as if we were the employer. In other words, what are the employer's concerns about an applicant's past behaviors?

3

Employers' Major Fears

"Employers want to hire people who are honest,
trustworthy, reliable, loyal, and competent. It's that simple.
They are not in the charitable business of just hiring an
ex-offender because he or she needs a job."

EMPLOYERS TODAY WANT WHAT they have always wanted from their employees – strong skills and abilities to do the job. But they also report placing higher value on **soft skills** associated with productive workplace behavior. They need employees to be at work and on time, eager to get things done, focused, cooperative, enthusiastic, motivated, responsive, and loyal.

Above all, employers want honesty, dependability, and value in exchange for the wages they pay. The good news is that many employers who hire ex-offenders find such qualities among those they employ. For them, giving someone a second chance is not an act of charity. It's simply the right thing to do, because it results in acquiring someone who is exceptionally enthusiastic, motivated, appreciative, and loyal. But there also are other "hiring an ex-offender" stories that are not so positive, which are all about taking risks and becoming disappointed and discouraged.

And that's exactly what you need to communicate to employers during your job search – taking a **risk** in hiring you will yield many benefits, because you are a person with desirable **skills** who understands and delivers **value** to the employer. Indeed, you are exceptionally motivated, dependable, loyal, and grateful, and you're prepared to demonstrate such qualities.

Apprehension and Disappointment

Employers are more apprehensive than ever when interviewing and screening applicants for jobs. Experience tells them that what they initially see – on the resume, application, or in the job interview – is not always what they get once they hire an individual.

In the past, many employers found out too late that applicants had lied about their educational background, the jobs they held in the past, the skills they possessed, their accomplishments on past jobs, or their criminal record. In other words, many employers realize they have been literally conned by people who made all kinds of untruthful verbal statements and promises during their job interview. Job applicants who made excuses for their past behavior and promised they had "changed their ways" repeated their past behavior and mistakes once they were on the job. Some of the blame can be placed squarely on the shoulders of a naive employer who failed to do a thorough background check concerning the individual's workplace behavior. Consequently, the employer was left to deal with the problems created by their own bad hiring, which resulted in a job vacancy to fill – again.

Employers want to better **predict** what your on-the-job performance is likely to be in **their** company or organization. Most believe the best predictor of your **future behavior** is your **past behavior**. This poses a problem for you if your past is full of red flags that scream, *"I am likely to be a bad risk – you'd be crazy to hire me!"*

Many employers will prefer to play it safe and hire applicants who don't bring a lot of negative baggage with them. But don't despair. It is possible to overcome a red flag background. However, it will take some effort on your part. I will provide guidelines a bit later that should help you turn red flags into green lights as you interview in an honest, yet positive, manner.

Cautious Employers

More than ever before, employers are conducting background checks to verify the information applicants put on their resumes or job applications as well as answers they provide during the job interview. This credentials check may go beyond calling the references supplied by the applicant and contacting previous employers. Many employers today will hire an independent firm to conduct a background investigation that may cover sensitive issues that cannot be legally addressed during a job interview as well as questions that a job applicant may lie about. These areas may include questions about an applicant's criminal background, marital status, family history, credit history, health issues, insurance claims, and legal suits. Employers are conducting more background checks today than in the past, because it's so easy and inexpensive to do so on the Internet and because they have been burned by dishonest applicants in the past. For just $19.95 employers can go online and get a great deal of background information on you within seconds! In fact, you might want to contact leading firms, such as everify.com, backgroundreport360.com, and backgroundchecks.com, to find out what information is readily available on you from these sources. One conclusion is inevitable – don't lie since there's no place to hide these days given the rise of big data on so many important aspects of our lives.

> *The best predictor of your future behavior is your past behavior – not what you say but what you have done, your pattern of behavior.*

Employers may administer a variety of pre-employment tests to determine an applicant's "fit" for the job. From aptitude tests and drug tests to personality profiles, psychological tests, or even a polygraph examination, an interviewer may make use of a number of instruments to better assess an applicant's qualifications and truthfulness.

So What Does An Employer Want From Me?

The following list includes 40 positive personality traits that are important to today's workplace. These are personality characteristics that employers look for and view as desirable traits in job applicants.

Here's what you need to do. In the blank space to the **left** of each characteristic, place a check mark next to those traits you honestly think you possess and that you believe others would use to describe you. No wishful thinking here – just be as honest with yourself as possible since you want to get accurate results that can help you with your job search. The only one you can cheat here is yourself.

Positive Workplace Personality Traits

Dependable		Discreet	
Cooperative		Flexible	
Attentive		Sensitive	
Focused		Honest	
Purposeful		Sincere	
Loyal		Effective	
Predictable		Efficient	
Talented		Precise	
Enthusiastic		Diligent	
Trustworthy		Versatile	
Intelligent		Perceptive	
Positive		Tactful	
Problem-solver		Astute	
Conscientious		Patient	
Motivated		Tenacious	
Reliable		Receptive	
Resourceful		Organized	
Responsible		Adaptive	
Literate		Successful	
Articulate		Respectful	

Notice the blank space to the **right** of each personality characteristic. In this space place a number between 5 and 1. A "five" means you believe you score very high on this characteristic; a "one" means you would score yourself very low. Use the numbers in between 5 and 1 that best describe how strongly you believe you possess each of the characteristics.

After completing this exercise, you need to ask yourself why you scored low on any particular characteristic that's important to employers. Next, you need to think about what you might do to "raise" your score in another three months.

Which of these characteristics are most important to your future employer varies with the job to be done, but most employers place an especially high value on employees being: **dependable, cooperative, loyal, predictable, trustworthy, motivated, reliable, responsible, discreet, and honest**. How did you rate yourself on these characteristics? What can you do to make improvements in those areas where you rated yourself low? Of course employers would like their employees to be talented, intelligent, and possess many of the other characteristics listed here. Can you, for example, demonstrate to an employer the following?

❑ He or she can count on you to be at work and on time each day
❑ He or she can count on you to focus your attention on getting the work done
❑ He or she can count on you to be honest and trustworthy
❑ He or she can count on you to cooperate with your supervisor and fellow employees

If so, you will have done much to put his or her mind at ease about how well you can function in the work environment.

Of course employers want to hire someone who has the **skills** to do the job, and you will need to demonstrate your work abilities as well, but even if you can do the job, the further question is, "*Will you?*" How **motivated** are you to do the job well from one day to the next?

Predicting Your Behavior

– Dependability –

Employers want to hire people who have a background of consistent, dependable, and competent performance. Before hiring you, they want to predict your future performance

> *You need to show proof that you have transformed your life. Talk is nice but cheap – it's not proof.*

based on an understanding of your past patterns of behavior. If you approach an employer with red flags in your background, you'll need to convince him or her that you have made changes in your life so that your future will not be a repeat performance of your past.

You have to do more than just be a fast-talking ex-con who engages in conning others with lies and half-truths. You need to **show proof** that you have transformed your life and that you will be an exceptionally good employee. Where's your proof? Not a 30-second pitch on the "new you." Who will stand by you and tell the truth about the "new you"? Not your self-serving relative, close friend, or faith-based advisor, who may lack credibility in the eyes of employers. For useful guidance on how to tell this new truth, please refer to Chapter 7 ("Tell the Truth About the New You") in my companion book, ***The Ex-Offender's Re-Entry Success Guide*** (Impact Publications, 2016).

Here's how employers think and calculate when making rational hiring decisions. *"Will you do the job I hire you to do?"* is a different question than *"Can you do the job?"* The first question deals with **motivation** while the second question deals with **skills**. Both skills and motivation are important to a possible employer. A major question in the employer's mind is, *"Will you be dependable?"* Even if you can do the job, but you don't show up for work – whether it is because you didn't hear your alarm go off, because you're hung over from a recurring substance abuse problem, or because you have been re-arrested and are back in jail – the work doesn't get done. Why you are not at work is usually not the main issue; the issue is that you are not there, and because you are not there the work isn't being done.

Example

A publisher I know had an employee who worked in the warehouse. Allison checked in books that came into the warehouse from other publishers and she pulled the books and packed books to be shipped out to clients who had placed orders for them. She did a great job when she showed up for work. She was one of the fastest workers the company had and her error rate was one of the lowest. In other words, she rarely shipped a wrong book by mistake.

Ideal employee? She could have been. But her attendance record was terrible. Her employer never knew whether she would show up for work or not. Much of her absent time was ostensibly because of illness. But whether her reasons for missing work were legitimate or not made little difference to the employer. The bottom line was the company's performance – work was not getting done, and the employer could not depend on her to be at work the next day either. So with reluctance, the employee had to let Allison go. Even though she could do the work, and did the work in an exemplary fashion when she showed up for work, she was fired because her long-term work pattern was one of undependability. The employer could not depend on her to be there to get the work accomplished.

– *Cooperation With Co-Workers* –

Employers want to hire a worker who will get along well with others. They want someone who will fit into the organization and not be a trouble maker. So interpersonal skills are an important consideration in making a hiring decision. Simply doing the work is not enough if the new employee creates more problems in the process.

Example

Alex seemed to be a great applicant when he interviewed for a job with a small family owned print shop. He had experience operating many of the presses the print shop used and would need very little training on any of the equipment. There was every reason to expect he would be a good hire. However, he had not been on the job very long before problems began – not with the presses, but with the people. Before long it was apparent that Alex had a serious problem with anger management and was unable to accept responsibility for any problem that took place on the shop floor. When he forgot to set one of the presses he was operating to stop printing when the customer's 500 copies had been run, he got angry at a co-worker and tried to blame him for the costly error. When another worker shouted for him to move out of the way because a heavy load was being wheeled through the plant, he shouted back that he'd stand anywhere he pleased and would not budge. After a few more similar incidents it was apparent he was not a good fit for the workplace, and he was let go. He had the technical skills, but was lacking in people skills.

– Cooperates With Boss(es) by Listening and Following Orders –

Employers want to hire an individual who will pay attention to directions and follow orders given by the boss or supervisor(s). They do not want to hire someone who rebels against authority, won't follow orders, or is unable to work with others cooperatively in the workplace. Indeed, the inability to listen, follow orders, and cooperate with supervisors are frequent reasons individuals get fired.

Example

Matt had a good job working with an installation crew operated by one of Cincinnati's best landscape companies. Employees who stayed with the company for a few years received generous raises and moved into more responsible positions. The company was especially proud of its talented and loyal workforce. Supervisors worked closely with their crews to ensure that everything got done according to plan and on time.

After six months on the job, Matt began to exhibit some troubling workplace behaviors. In addition to frequently coming to work late, he had trouble following instructions. A pattern was starting to emerge that came to a head on Thursday afternoon when a job had to be redone because of Matt's inability to listen and follow instructions. It wasn't pretty.

When clearly instructed where and how to plant a wall of 60 blue junipers, Matt managed to plant them too deeply and in a most unattractive pattern. His supervisor came over and just shook his head and said *"Matt, that's not what I told you to do. Look at this plan again. You were supposed follow it carefully. Here's how they need to be arranged on the hillside. Also, you planted them too deeply. They will be dead within a month! You should know better. We've done several similar jobs over the past few months. What's wrong with you?"* Matt got angry and blurted out *"Your directions were crap, your plan was stupid, and I don't remember how deep I'm suppose to plant these things. And that's Pete's job. So get off my ass!"*

Well, the supervisor immediately got off of Matt's butt by getting his ass out of there – he fired Matt right on the spot for insubordination and stupidity. Matt is now looking for another landscape job, or something else he thinks he might be good at doing. The good thing is that he doesn't have to get up at 5am every day, a real problem when stay out late at night with you buddies. He's also dealing with a relapse issue (alcohol) that contributed to his erratic behavior and angry outburst. His head is a bit screwed up right now, but he's going to soldier on with a new resume and hopefully find a new job soon. He's going to check out some temporary employment firms tomorrow. In the meantime, his money is running out and he's not sure what he's going to do next month if things don't turn around. Matt is still very angry about getting fired. He thinks they should have fired the stupid supervisor!

– Trustworthy –

Employers want to hire an individual they can trust. They want someone whom they can trust not to steal from them or other employees; trust them not to "fudge" the hours worked on a time card; trust them not to use alcohol or illegal substances in the workplace; trust them not to share "privileged information" (company secrets) where applicable, with people outside the company.

Example

A few weeks after Brad was hired, his boss began to think he had made a hiring mistake. He just couldn't trust Brad. He frequently came to work late or missed work altogether. When he did come to work he goofed off much of the time, and had conversations with co-workers which took their time away from doing work as well. On top of that, he frequently received personal calls on company time. Office supplies seemed to be disappearing and other employees began losing some of their personal belongings. Although no one could prove that Brad was stealing, since the losses began soon after he started work he was certainly suspect. The bottom line – no one at work trusted Brad. The boss fired him and regretted that he had not let him go sooner.

Employers Want Value for the Wages They Pay

Employers are apprehensive that even if they successfully identify an individual with the skills to do the job, they may make a mistake in hiring because the job applicant may be lacking in positive workplace personality traits. Why are they afraid of making a bad hiring decision? Because it has happened to them before! The person who indicated during the interview that he had the skills to do the job was a disaster after he was hired.

In the examples above, one employee who did good work when she showed up didn't show up for work much of the time. Another employee couldn't get along with other workers or with the boss. Yet another employee stole things from the workplace. In each case the employer had no choice but to fire the employee and start the hiring process all over again. This costs both time and money. Now each of these employers is both angry and scared. He is angry at the employee he had to fire for lying to him; he is angry at himself for letting himself be conned by someone who wanted to collect a paycheck without giving value in return; and he is afraid it will happen again with another potential employee.

Can you try to put yourself in the place of the employer and understand the apprehensions he has as he begins the hiring process all over again? If not, go back and re-read the examples from the perspective of an employer rather than a employee. Why should you hire and keep someone with such workplace behaviors?

Understand the Employer's Viewpoint

Consider the following situations/questions to determine your understanding of the employer's point of view and the dilemma the employer faces.

1. **If a candidate for a job has the skills to do the job, why should the employer worry about anything else?**

   _____

   _____

   _____

   _____

2. **What are three other things, in addition to the skills to do the job, the employer wants in an employee?**

   1. _____

   2. _____

   3. _____

   4. _____

3. **Why does the employer care whether I stay with the company for only a few weeks or months?**

   _____

   _____

   _____

4. **Give an example of a situation when an employer might be suspicious of my motives (think I might be conning him) when I go for a job interview?**

   _____

   _____

   _____

5. **What positive workplace characteristics can I truthfully communicate to employers?** Go back to the list of Positive Workplace Personality Traits on page 13 to help make your selection. Look at the space to the right of each trait where you placed a number between 5 and 1. Pay special attention to those traits you rated as a 5 or 4. These are the traits you thought were your strongest. List five of your strongest traits below. Just

list the traits in the underlined space indicated as number 1 thru 5. Don't fill in the spaces for examples yet.

POSITIVE TRAIT #1 _____

    Example: _____

_____

_____

    Example: _____

_____

_____

POSITIVE TRAIT #2 _____

    Example: _____

_____

_____

    Example: _____

_____

_____

POSITIVE TRAIT #3 _____

    Example: _____

_____

_____

    Example: _____

_____

_____

POSITIVE TRAIT #4 _____

    Example: _____

_____

_____

    Example: _____

_____

_____

POSITIVE TRAIT #5 _____

    Example: _____

    _____

    _____

    Example: _____

    _____

    _____

Red Flag Behaviors Beyond Illegal Behaviors

Have you noticed that in each of the situations discussed, none of the employee problems relate directly to time spent in prison? In other words, employers have a lot of problems with on-the-job behaviors of people who have **not** been convicted of a crime! Your background may include red flag behaviors in some of these other areas in addition to your criminal activities. Or, even though you are an ex-offender, you may score high on many of the positive workplace personality traits employers value. But the interviewer won't know about these positive traits unless you are prepared to talk about them in a **focused way**. The important thing is to highlight the areas that you can promote as your **strengths** as you participate in the give and take of a job interview.

As you put yourself in the employer's position and try to think like an employer, anticipate his concerns and choose examples that demonstrate he can count on you to be better than the average employee in several important areas, such as dependability, reliability, responsibleness, trustworthiness, honesty, or cooperation.

Don't feel you need to talk about all the character traits that employers value. That would be overkill and likely sound less than believable that you excel in all of them. In Question #5 on page 18, you selected five traits that you believe are your strongest. Now try to recall an example or two of something you have done that would demonstrate each of these traits.

If you can choose positive examples of something you have done to demonstrate these traits from "on the job" situations, that will be your strongest support, but you need not limit yourself to job-related examples if you either have none or have better ones from other areas of your life. Go back and fill in the spaces marked "Example" for each of the five traits you selected.

So What If You Are an Ex-Offender?

When you face the job interview with a conviction and time in prison behind you, your potential red flags are of concern to the employer beyond the more general problem behaviors we have looked at thus far. Employers are looking for individuals who have a positive predictable pattern of performance. A prison record suggests a pattern that if repeated, predicts problems for a future employer.

Ask yourself, why would an employer hire an individual whose past red flags suggest the probability that trouble could spill over to the workplace? If you committed a crime in the past and it related to the workplace, such as stealing or assault, an employer may assume you may commit a similar crime in the future as well as affect the morale of fellow employees who may worry about your history of criminal behavior and their safety. Since employers have certain legal responsibilities to operate a safe and secure workplace, they can't afford to take such risks. After all, if something happens to an employee because of you, the employer can be sued for operating an unsafe workplace. Indeed, many employers have ended up with $1+ million court judgments against them, because they hired an ex-offender who injured fellow employees. While some ex-offenders are bonded, nonetheless, the safety/security issue looms large in the minds of employers who simply don't want to – and frankly don't need to – take such unnecessary changes.

Even if the crime you committed was totally unrelated to the workplace, if you are hired and later commit another crime and are then arrested, it affects your employer because you will then not be at work to do your job. The employer is left with the work you were expected to do not getting done, and he has to go through the hiring and training of another person to replace you. This costs the employer time and money.

If you are to overcome this looming red flag, you will need to acknowledge responsibility for your previous act(s) and present a convincing case that your behavior has significantly changed since your conviction. In other words, you need to convince the employer that you will not commit another offense; you will not let the employer down. Take very seriously the need to do this successfully. Your future employment depends on it. Next, we'll turn our attention to strategies you can use to deal with the very real fear the employer is likely to have about "taking a chance" hiring an ex-offender.

4

Turn Your Red Flags Into Green Lights

"Those who first recognize their red flags and then learn to turn them into green lights will conquer one of the major challenges facing ex-offenders."

THE THREE MOST IMPORTANT things as you get ready for a job interview are **preparation, preparation, and preparation**. I cannot overstate the importance of being prepared. Some job seekers think they can't prepare, because they don't know what the questions will be, while others are just too lazy to spend the time to prepare. They think they can just talk there way through a job interview with ease.

Yes, you can anticipate **most** of what will happen in a job interview, anticipate the likely concerns an employer will have about your background, and prepare to do your very best in the interview. This is the rest of your life we're talking about. Isn't it worth your time and effort to prepare to do the very best you can during the interview? You absolutely **must** prepare if you want to present yourself well. And presenting your best self is critical to getting a job offer.

I want you to be yourself, but I also want you to be your **best self**. That is what preparation is all about. It's a lot easier to think about your responses to questions or consider what points you want to make about your background ahead of time, rather than when you are under the stress you are likely to feel during the job interview. You **can anticipate and prepare** for most, if not all, of the questions you will be asked during your job interviews.

Identify Your Personal Red Flags

You know whether you have things in your past that are likely to raise questions and concerns in the mind of potential employers. Let's review several that were mentioned earlier:

1. Applicant has no high school diploma (or GED)
2. Applicant had poor grades in school

3. Applicant has little or no work experience
4. Applicant was fired from a previous job
5. Applicant has a pattern of job-hopping
6. Applicant has poor references
7. Applicant has a criminal record

While these are some of the most common bases for employer objections, you may have something in your background that is not listed here but which you know may create questions in the mind of an employer.

So start by doing an honest assessment of your past behaviors that might negatively affect your employability. Some of these behaviors will deal with the crime you were convicted of committing. Include these, but go beyond behaviors relating to your crime(s). Include all the major behaviors (things you have done in your past) that might raise concern in the mind of an employer – if he knew about them. For example, what bad habits might you have that would not knock you out of consideration for the job as well as pose difficulties once you're on the job?

Begin this activity on page 24. We'll focus on 11 of your most critical red flags that could affect your employability. Identify next to each red flag behavior number one of the major things you have done that you believe will be a red flag to an employer. To get started, go back to the list of 10 red flags you made on pages 9-10. Do all of the behaviors you listed there still seem to be potential "knockouts" if/when the employer finds out about them? Are there others you can think of now that you did not list earlier?

Remember, you want to be **honest but not stupid** when dealing with the information exchanged during the job interview. In other words, you don't want to lie to the employer, and you don't want to hide (withhold) information that might get you fired if the employer finds out about it later – after you have been hired. Withholding information about your red flags could also potentially knock you out of consideration for the job if the employer knew about it all along and was testing you to see whether you would be honest about it or hears about it from one of your references when those are checked.

The interview is your chance to **sell yourself** for the job. You must promote yourself – honestly, but in the most positive way possible. This is what your preparation should focus on doing. In the case of red flag behaviors, it means being honest (but not stupid) about your past mistakes, but convincing the employer you are no longer a risky hire based on your past mistakes. You demonstrate you are not making untrue promises just to get the job (conning him). To convince him of your honesty and sincerity, you must support your change of behaviors by:

1. Taking responsibility for your past actions that got you into trouble
2. Indicating you understand why he would be concerned about the past action that got you into trouble (your understanding of an employer's point of view)

3. Indicating what changes you have made in your situation so that the negative behavior will not occur again

4. Indicating how long it has been (if a significant length of time) since the offending behavior took place

5. Stressing your determination to never engage in the offending behavior again

For now, start by just listing your red flag behaviors on the numbered lines. List the most important ones from pages 9-10 as well as any additional ones you think of now. Skip the lines marked "A" and "B" and leave those blank for now. We will come back to those later. List **all** the major red flag knockout things you can think of. If you take a shortcut and omit some, they may relate to questions you are later asked in an interview and you may not be prepared with good responses. That could keep you from getting the job.

---

1. RED FLAG BEHAVIOR #1 _____

    A. Give reason(s) why the behavior listed above happened.

       _____

       _____

       _____

       _____

    B. Indicate what has changed in the situation/why you will not repeat this behavior.

       _____

       _____

       _____

       _____

    C. Strategy/Gist Notes.

       _____

       _____

       _____

       _____

2. RED FLAG BEHAVIOR #2 _____

A. Give reason(s) why the behavior listed above happened.

_____

_____

_____

_____

B. Indicate what has changed in the situation/why you will not repeat this behavior.

_____

_____

_____

_____

C. Strategy/Gist Notes.

_____

_____

_____

_____

3. RED FLAG BEHAVIOR #3 _____

A. Give reason(s) why the behavior listed above happened.

_____

_____

_____

_____

B. Indicate what has changed in the situation/why you will not repeat this behavior.

_____

_____

_____

_____

C. Strategy/Gist Notes.

_____

_____

_____

_____

4. RED FLAG BEHAVIOR #4 _____

A. Give reason(s) why the behavior listed above happened.

_____

_____

_____

_____

B. Indicate what has changed in the situation/why you will not repeat this behavior.

_____

_____

_____

_____

C. Strategy/Gist Notes.

_____

_____

_____

_____

5. RED FLAG BEHAVIOR #5 _____

    A. Give reason(s) why the behavior listed above happened.

_____

_____

_____

_____

    B. Indicate what has changed in the situation/why you will not repeat this behavior.

_____

_____

_____

_____

    C. Strategy/Gist Notes.

_____

_____

_____

_____

6. RED FLAG BEHAVIOR #6 _____

    A. Give reason(s) why the behavior listed above happened.

_____

_____

_____

_____

B. Indicate what has changed in the situation/why you will not repeat this behavior.

_____

_____

_____

_____

C. Strategy/Gist Notes.

_____

_____

_____

_____

---

7. RED FLAG BEHAVIOR #7 _____

A. Give reason(s) why the behavior listed above happened.

_____

_____

_____

_____

B. Indicate what has changed in the situation/why you will not repeat this behavior.

_____

_____

_____

_____

C. Strategy/Gist Notes.

_____

_____

_____

_____

8. RED FLAG BEHAVIOR #8 _____

    A. Give reason(s) why the behavior listed above happened

_____

_____

_____

_____ .

    B. Indicate what has changed in the situation/why you will not repeat this behavior.

_____

_____

_____

_____

    C. Strategy/Gist Notes.

_____

_____

_____

_____

9. RED FLAG BEHAVIOR #9 _____

    A. Give reason(s) why the behavior listed above happened.

_____

_____

_____

_____

   B. **Indicate what has changed in the situation/why you will not repeat this behavior.**

_____

_____

_____

_____

   C. **Strategy/Gist Notes.**

_____

_____

_____

_____

10. RED FLAG BEHAVIOR #10 _____

   A. Give reason(s) why the behavior listed above happened.

_____

_____

_____

_____

   B. **Indicate what has changed in the situation/why you will not repeat this behavior.**

_____

_____

_____

_____

   C. **Strategy/Gist Notes.**

_____

_____

_____

_____

---

11. RED FLAG BEHAVIOR #11 _____

   A. Give reason(s) why the behavior listed above happened.

_____

_____

_____

_____

   B. Indicate what has changed in the situation/why you will not repeat this behavior.

_____

_____

_____

_____

   C. Strategy/Gist Notes.

_____

_____

_____

_____

Next, go back to each red flag behavior you have listed and write down the reason(s) why each happened in the spaces marked "A". Let's say, for example, that one of your red flag behaviors is that you were fired from a previous job. You would write that down on one of the numbered lines. So now that you have written down all the red flag behaviors that you can think of that apply to you, go back and begin answering Part A for each behavior.

Here, the question is why the behavior happened. If you were fired from a job, why were you fired? Was it because you didn't show up for work or showed up late? Was it because you didn't get along with your boss or your co-workers? Was it because you wouldn't follow orders? Did you steal from your employer or lie to him? **Are you going to repeat these behaviors with your next employer?** Because if you are, no one will want to be your next employer.

Does your employment record indicate you are a job hopper? Why? Why have you had so many jobs over a relatively short period of time? Remember, when you are looking at the time you have spent in various jobs that you need to look at this from an **employer's** point of view – not yours. Three jobs in a year may not seem unreasonable to you, but changing jobs every three or four months will certainly raise questions in the employer's mind. **If I hire you, are you going to repeat this pattern of behavior and leave after three or four months?**

Do you have a criminal record? Why? What did you do? **Are you likely to repeat the behavior that got you convicted?** Have you ever had a problem with drugs or alcohol? Why? **Are you really rehabilitated, or are there likely to be problems that will affect your work on your next job?**

It's important that you address each of these red flag behaviors as honestly as possible. Making excuses or blaming others for your problem is often a sign of a more serious behavioral problem that most likely affects your relationships with employers, co-workers, clients, family, and friends – not taking responsibility for your actions. Taking responsibility for your past actions, especially the negative ones you may wish had never happened – is the first step to making changes in your behavior and hence in your life. Employers have heard all the excuses before, and the lame ones just won't cut it with most job interviewers. So step up and take responsibility. After the recognition of a problem behavior, taking responsibility is the next step toward making a positive change.

So if you have not already done this, go back and fill in the "why" sections (marked "A") for each of the red flag behaviors you have listed. If you have already completed this part, we suggest that you go back to it again – right now – and read what you have written. Is there anything you wrote that you wish to add to or change? Go ahead; now is your chance to make changes if you wish.

Questions That Follow Red Flags

You have probably noticed a pattern here. When a red flag is raised, the next question in the employer's mind is why? Why did you engage in that behavior? The question that invariably follows the *"Why?"* question in the employer's mind is, *"Are you going to repeat that behavior – are you going to do it again?"* These follow-up questions, *"Why?"* and *"Will you do it again?,"* may or may not be posed verbally, but they are definitely on the employer's mind. So you will need to respond to these questions – whether or not they are actually asked – if you want to have a chance at getting the job.

Prepare to Lower the Red Flag

Remember, the employer is looking for knockout factors – things that make him or her decide not to take a chance with you. The employer takes a chance with every new employee hired. So you need to consider the employer's concerns about your background, and then truthfully promote yourself by responding to these concerns in an honest, but positive, way.

Why were you fired? If you were fired because you were frequently absent or late for work, we assume you wrote that down. But this raises the follow-up "why"question. Why were you absent or late for work so often? Was it because you were often out late the night before? Okay, why were you out late the night, before if you had to go to work the next day? Were you partying late into the night or were you working a second job and had the night shift? Or were you also a student and you were studying late into the night?

In this example, no matter what the reason for the employee's absence or tardiness, the result for the employer was the same. The employee's behavior created problems in the workplace. Either work did not get done or someone else had to do it.

Now that you have responded to as many "whys" as the situation is likely to raise in the mind of an employer, go on to the third part for each red flag behavior – Part B. Why will this behavior not be repeated again? As you look at the possible responses suggested above for the employee being absent or late for work, it may at first look to you like only one – out partying late the night before – is not excusable.

Whoa there; you are thinking like the employee – not the employer! Even though "out partying" probably looks worse than the other reasons to an employer, remember, to the employer, if the work does not get done because the employee is constantly late or absent, the excuse doesn't really matter. The bottom line is the same: either the work did not get done, or someone else had to do it – taking that person away from the work he or she was scheduled to do.

So the employer you are interviewing with wants to know that your red flag behavior – whatever it is – has changed. Without reasons to support your assertion as to why the behavior has changed, you are likely to be viewed as simply trying to con the employer into hiring you.

Ask yourself what things in your situation have truly changed since you engaged in the problem behavior. What truthful things can you tell the employer to help convince him that you no longer are engaging in, nor will you engage in the red flag behavior? Read the following two examples. After you have done that, we'll ask you go back and fill in Part B, which asks you to indicate what changes you have made in your situation to assure others, such as a potential employer, that you are unlikely to resume the red flag behavior.

1. Red flag behavior #1: I was arrested along with several friends who were in the car with me and convicted of possession with the intent to sell illegal drugs.

A. Give reason(s) why the behavior listed above happened.

I fell in with the wrong crowd and wanted to fit in. I knew there were drugs in the car, but went along with what the others were doing. And although it took some time before I was ready to admit it, I was guilty of the crime and deserved the sentence I received.

B. Indicate what has changed in the situation/why you will not do it again.

While serving my time in prison, I had a lot of time on my hands to think about what had happened to me – the trouble I had gotten myself into. At first, I told myself (and others) that I hadn't known the drugs were in the car – that I was innocent and was wrongfully arrested. But eventually, in part as a result of some group sessions in prison during which I was confronted with my behavior, I came to the point that I admitted my involvement in the situation. I was determined that once I was released, I never would return to prison. I was fortunate to have a great counselor who helped me plan a course of action for when I was released. He suggested I complete the work for my GED and recommended me for a job at the prison so I could get work experience. My supervisor for the job I had at the prison has given me a good recommendation. An important part of the plan involved moving to another suburb when I was released, so I would not come into daily contact with the guys from the crowd I had been running with when I got into trouble.

I have followed the plan we put together and believe I have made a lot of positive changes in my life. I no longer run with the crowd that got me into trouble, and the friends I have now are a positive force in my life.

Analysis. Note several things the potential employee has done:

1. He frankly and truthfully explained the situation.

2. He took responsibility for his actions and has accepted the punishment he received.

3. He took steps to improve his future employability – completed the GED and got work experience while he was in prison as well as earned a good recommendation.

4. He made a change in his living situation so he would not come into contact with the individuals who might lure him into future trouble.

This individual has a good chance of being hired if he has the skills to do the job. He has not only taken responsibility for his actions, but has taken steps to improve his employability while he was in prison and to remove himself from a potential bad situation once he was released.

2. Red flag behavior #2: I was fired from my job at XYZ Motor Repair.

A. Give reason(s) why the behavior listed above happened.

I showed up for work late too many days and my boss fired me.

B. Indicate what has changed in the situation/why you will not do it again.

I realize it is not a good excuse that I was late for work so often, and that my boss had to have someone he could count on to be at work so the job could get done. At the same time this happened I was working a second job and I got off work from the one job at 1:00am. I was supposed to start work at my second job at 6:00am. Taking the commute time for both jobs into consideration, which totaled about an hour, that left about three and a half hours for sleep each night. After a few weeks, the lack of sleep caught up with me, and I am afraid I let my employer down.

I can assure you that it will not happen again. I had taken the second job to help pay off some loans. That debt is now taken care of, and I am able to live within my means. I assure you that if you hire me, you will find me to be a responsible employee whom you can count on. I realize the importance of being on the job each day and on time in order that the work gets done.

Analysis. Notice what the potential employee has done as he addresses the second situation:

1. He frankly and truthfully explained the situation.

2. He noted that he understood his employer needed a worker who was on time for work each day.

3. He respected his former employer's decision by not making excuses or negative comments about the employer who fired him.

4. He takes responsibility by explaining why he was late, what corrective actions he took, and notes the situation he was in at the time no longer exists.

5. He again stresses his understanding of the employer's needs – an employee who is on the job each day and on time so that the work gets done.

This employee, even though he was fired from a previous job, has a good chance of being hired if he has the skills to do the job he has applied for, because he has said the right things to make the prospective employer believe he understands why he was fired, holds no bad feelings toward the former employer who fired him, and has indicated how his situation has changed. The situation that created the former problem no longer exists.

Now, you should be ready to go back and fill in Part B. How has the situation around each red flag behavior changed in ways you can use to convince a skeptical person – a potential employer – that your situation is different now. These changes in your situation make it more believable that your change in behavior will continue. Fill in the blanks in Part B before you continue.

If you have completed both parts A and B for each of your personal red flag behaviors, you should be ready to move ahead. You have now identified your personal red flag behaviors, the reason(s) why the behavior took place, and what has changed about your situation so you can demonstrate the behavior will not happen again.

Plan the "Gist" of Your Explanations

You are ready to formulate the "gist" of the responses or comments you will make to the prospective employer about your personal red flag situations – Part C. The concept of

Don't try to memorize your responses. If you do, you'll probably forget your lines and you'll sound insincere. You need to plan the "gist" of your response and appear genuine.

the "gist" is very simple – you have a **summary strategy** for talking about your red flag. In other words, jot down exactly how you plan to explain your red flag. Planning the "gist" does not mean that you are going to memorize a response or comment. If you did that, you would appear less than genuine in your response. Instead, by planning your "gist," you are deciding the general way in which you will talk about this particular aspect of your life. You'll emphasize the main points you need to stress in your response. You'll know what you need to say and you'll sound unrehearsed and thus authentic.

Ask yourself what you can say to the employer that is honest, yet positive, about how you handled or are handling the situation now. Remember to take responsibility. In so doing, it's important that you explain what has changed or what you did to change your situation. It is the change that both demonstrates your commitment to the change and the likelihood that the changed behavior will continue in the future. In doing this, you reveal some important elements in your character that are desired by employers – honesty, integrity, responsibility, and change.

Again, you should plan the "gist" of your responses/comments you want to make to an employer for each of the red flag situations you have identified. **Don't try to memorize it word for word**. If you memorize, chances are you will forget it (especially in a stressful interview situation) or it will sound canned or both. Neither will be convincing to the employer. Be familiar with the "gist" of what you want to say and be ready to convey that to the employer in the words that come naturally to you when you are in the interview. You want to convey the following positive qualities in your response:

- what **changed** in your situation
- what you have done to **overcome** the negative behavior
- what you have **learned** from the experience

In the example we have been following of the applicant who had been fired by his boss at XYZ Motors, the situation had changed in that he was now only working one job rather than two. His former situation had him trying to manage on 3½ hours of sleep a night. Now he could get a full night's sleep and get up in time to be at work on time. He had learned how important it is to the employer to have workers on the job each day and on time so that the work gets done.

Keep the following things in mind as you plan your "gist" response or comments:

- **Advice #1:** There are many different ways to tell the truth. Keep it honest, but not stupid. Tell the truth in the most positive manner possible, but do not confess more than is necessary.

  Avoid: Blurting out all your weaknesses or negatives. The job interview is not the time nor place for "true confessions." Keep your comments related to the work situation. Your situation at home, as long as it does not affect the work you are doing, is none of the employer's business.

- **Advice: #2:** Keep your comments concise, focused, and to the point.

  Avoid: Talking too much, rambling on and on out of nervousness. A little silence is all right.

We have discussed planning the "gist" of your responses to questions the interviewer may ask. If you believe the employer may be hesitant about something in your background, but he isn't asking you about it, you can bring it up yourself. If you have a positive explanation for a red flag behavior, why would you leave that hesitancy in the employer's mind? It will likely grow as a negative factor as the employer weighs your candidacy against other applicants for the job. You not only can, but should, bring it up if you believe you have a positive explanation that will help your chances.

> *"You're aware that I was fired from XYZ Motors. I would like to explain the situation and what I have done to make sure this never happens again."*

If you are going to bring up a red flag behavior, don't wait until the end of the interview to do so, and you certainly don't want to begin with it either. The beginning and the end of the interview are most likely to be remembered with greater clarity by the employer. So try to end on the most positive note possible.

Now, let's revisit the activity on red flag behaviors one more time. Please go back to pages 24-31. The information you have already formulated for each red flag behavior should help you as you consider the "gist" (or strategy) of how you would talk about each red flag behavior if either you or the employer were to bring it up during a job interview. Jot down some notes in the spaces provided marked Part C.

5

40 Interview Mistakes Many Job Seekers Make

Other Red Flags You Should Avoid

---

*"Red flags also can arise anytime during the interview.
Make a few of these and your other red flags
may not make much difference!"*

LET'S PUT THIS WHOLE job interview process in perspective by examining frequent interview mistakes job seekers make. Most of these errors have nothing to do with being an ex-offender or someone with a not-so-hot backgrounds. Most actually occur while the interview takes place. Not surprisingly, job seekers make numerous interview errors, many of which employers think are "unbelievable," such as showing up late for the interview!

Like resume and letter errors, interview sins can quickly knock you out of the competition. They are **red flags** indicating you have "issues" that the employer does not wish to inherit. Unlike many other job search mistakes, interview errors tend to be both **unforgettable and unforgiving**. After all, this is the time when first impressions count the most. Make a bad first impression and the remaining minutes of your interview will be downhill and the door will permanently close behind you as you leave the interview.

Positive and Negative Goals of Employers

Employers have both positive and negative goals in mind. On the positive side, they want to hire someone who can do the job and add value or benefits to their organization. On the negative side, they are always looking for clues, or red flags, that tell them why they should **not** hire you. After all, they have made hiring mistakes before. For example, you may be another stranger who makes inflated claims about your competence, taking credit for others' accomplishments, in the hope of getting a job offer. Or perhaps you know little about the company (couldn't even find time to visit their website!), you ask about salary and benefits early in the job interview, or you fail to ask thoughtful questions – behaviors that usually indicate that a candidate is not really interested in the

38

work and thus not a good "fit" for the organization. And if you are too social and talk too much, you may be perceived as a potentially irritating hire. Who wants to listen to you talk all day long?

It's not until you start performing on the job that the employer gets to see the "real you" and discover your attitudes and patterns of behavior. In the meantime, the employer needs to be on his or her guard looking for evidence that you may be the wrong person for the job. Make a mistake during the job interview and you may be instantly eliminated from further consideration. Therefore, you must be on your very best behavior and avoid the many common mistakes interviewers report that interviewees often make in face-to-face interviews.

40 Killer Interview Mistakes

Whatever you do, try to avoid making any of the following interview errors. Committing one of these mistakes can instantly knock you out of the competition:

1. **Arrives late to the interview.** First impressions really do count and they are remembered for a long time. Arrive late and you've made one of the worst impressions possible! Indeed, regardless of what you say or do during the interview, you may never recover from this initial mistake. Employers wonder *"Will you also come to work late?"* You may think this doesn't happen often. Think again. Some employers report that nearly 50 percent of their candidates arrive late for the interview. Such candidates offer all kinds of excuses – from legitimate to inexcusable: overslept, ran out of gas, car broke down, illness in the family, got lost, involved in an accident, roads flooded, Mapquest gave inaccurate directions, navigation system failed. And here's the real killer excuse – *"I got lost because your directions weren't very clear."*

2. **Makes a bad impression in the waiting area.** Treats receptionists and secretaries as inferiors – individuals who may have important input into the hiring process when later asked by the interviewer or hiring manager *"What was your impression of this candidate?"* Caught reading frivolous materials – *People Magazine* – in the waiting area when company reports and related literature were readily available. Plays with technology – makes calls on cell phone, listens to iPod, plays with apps, and checks e-mail, Asks stupid questions and/or engages in embarrassing small talk and chews gum.

   Remember, this is an important time to look like a serious candidate to others who may see you and speak with you in the reception area. Don't make the mistake of believing that your interview begins once you meet the interviewer. It begins the moment you arrive at the interview site, which may be 15 minutes before the face-to-face interview session begins.

3. **Offers poor and unacceptable excuses for behavior.** Excuses are usually red flags indicating that a person is unwilling to take responsibility and do the work. Here are some excuses often heard during job interviews:

   ▪ *I forgot.*

   ▪ *It wasn't my fault.*

   ▪ *That's their problem.*

   ▪ *It was a bad company.*

   ▪ *My boss was a real jerk.*

   ▪ *The school wasn't very good.*

   ▪ *They told me to do it that way.*

   ▪ *I can't remember why I did that.*

   ▪ *No one there appreciated my work.*

   ▪ *I didn't have time to visit your website.*

   ▪ *I'm not a job hopper – I'm getting lots of experience.*

   The last two excuses can be very revealing. Surprisingly, many interviewees fail to do their homework and visit the website of a perspective employer. There's simply no excuse for failing to do this other than laziness or disinterest. If you don't have Internet access, you can always go to a public library and use the Internet for free. Library personnel will help you log on and find what you need to find. If you didn't have time to visit the website, then perhaps the employer doesn't have time to take you seriously. If you are a serial job hopper – averaging more than one job every one to two years – you better put together a very convincing story to dispel any suspicions that you are likely to leave this employer shortly, too. Lame excuses won't work. Why invest time and money in someone who plans to soon leave? Why would an employer want to train you for your next job with another employer? Do you know what it costs to replace an employee? One to two times your base salary! Job hoppers simply are not welcomed by many employers, other than ones who anticipate a high employee turnover in their industry, such as retail stores, restaurants, construction, and other low-wage blue-collar and service industry positions.

4. **Presents a poor appearance and negative image.** Dresses inappropriately for the interview – under-dresses or over-dresses for the position or the time of day. Offers a limp and sweaty handshake, emits irritating odors (from perfumes to bad breath and body odor), over-decorates with jewelry and body art (tattoos), looks extremely overweight, or appears too old or too young for the job. He or she may need to learn some basic grooming habits, from haircut and style to makeup and nails, or undergo a major makeover.

5. **Expresses bad, negative, and corrosive attitudes.** Tends to be negative, overbearing, extremely aggressive, cynical, and opinionated to the extreme. Expresses intolerance and strong prejudices toward others. Complains a lot about everything and everybody. Indicates a possible caustic personality that will not fit in well with the company. Regardless of how talented this person may be, unless he works in a cell by himself, he'll probably be fired within two months for having a bad attitude that pollutes the office and harms morale. **Attitude is everything** in a job interview. It reveals your motivation and enthusiasm to do the job as well as indicates how you probably make decisions and deal with others.

6. **Engages in inappropriate and unexpected behaviors for an interview situation.** Shows off scars, tattoos, muscles, or pictures of family. Slouches in the chair. Tells inappropriate jokes. Expresses extreme opinions. Picks up items on the interviewer's desk. Flirts with the interviewer. Possibly an exhibitionist who may also want to date the boss and harass co-workers!

7. **Appears somewhat incoherent and unfocused.** Tends to offer incomplete thoughts, loses focus, and jumps around to unrelated ideas. Hard to keep a focused conversation going. Incoherent thought processes indicate a possible attention deficit disorder (ADD) problem or some other disability, such as a drug or alcohol addiction, that could be detrimental to performing the job.

8. **Inarticulate.** Speaks poorly, from sound of voice and diction to grammar, vocalized pauses, and jargon. Uses lots of *"you know," "ah," "like," "okay,"* and *"well"* fillers. Expresses a low-class or age-inappropriate street language – *"cool," "damn," "man," "wow."* Not a good candidate for using the telephone or interacting with clients. Appears verbally illiterate or wired for failure.

9. **Gives short, incomplete, and/or vague and uncertain answers to questions.** Tends to respond to most questions with *"Yes," "No," "Maybe," "I'm not sure,"* or *"That's an interesting idea"* when the interviewer expects more in-depth and decisive answers. Appears shallow and indicates a lack of substance, initiative, interest, and enthusiasm. Indicates a high degree of uncertainly in making decisions – not a good action-oriented candidate who needs to make quick and smart decisions based on limited information.

10. **Lacks a sense of direction.** When asked where he sees himself five years from now, has difficulty giving a thoughtful answer. Appears to have no goals or apparent objectives beyond "a job." Apparently he is just looking for another job and paycheck rather than pursuing a passion or cause. Little indication the candidate is self-motivated. This one will probably watch the clock all day

long and require lots of close supervision and direction, which creates another unnecessary job!

11. **Appears ill or has a possible undisclosed medical condition.** Looks pale, glassy-eyed, gaunt, or yellow. Coughs, sneezes, and sounds terrible. Volunteers information about some past health issues and talks about his upcoming operation – within six weeks of starting the job! Suspects this person may have an illness or a drug and alcohol addiction that could be costly to the company and detrimental to doing the job.

12. **Volunteers personal information that normally would be illegal or inappropriate to ask.** Candidate makes interviewer feel uncomfortable by talking about religion, politics, age, family, divorce, sexual orientation, physical and mental health, or criminal history. Volunteers the fact that she hopes to soon start a family, she currently receives unemployment benefits, spouse is in jail, she is in the process of getting a divorce, or she is a single or unwed mother with two small children. In response to "tell me about yourself," the interviewee focuses almost solely on **personal** rather than professional matters – birthplace, schools, family, hobbies, sports interests, and travel plans. The interviewer finds all these facts "interesting" but of little relevance to the job in question. Some of the personal and lifestyle information raises red flags.

13. **Emits bad or irritating smells.** Reeks of excessive perfume, cologne, or shaving lotion – could kill mosquitos! Can smell smoke or alcohol on breath. Strong body odor indicates personal hygiene issues. Has bad breath throughout the interview, which gets cut short by the employer for an "unexplained" reason. Interviewer concludes this candidate just doesn't smell right for the job! He's sure fellow workers and clients would agree with his assessment.

14. **Shows little enthusiasm, drive, or initiative.** Appears to be just looking for a job, putting in time, and collecting a paycheck. Tends to be passive and indifferent most of the time and a self-centered wise guy some of the time. No evidence of being a self-starter who takes initiative and solves problems on his own. Not sure what motivates this person other than close supervision and possible threats of termination. Indeed, he'll require constant supervision and direction. The company will have an employee with lots of play-time on his hands or this will soon become a case where the job expands to fill the time allotted. He'll become the "job guy" who always says *"I did my job just like you told me,"* but not much beyond what's assigned. Don't expect much from this person, who will probably be overpaid for what he produces and who may create more problems that will need to be solved by other employees.

15. **Lacks confidence and self-esteem.** Seems unsure of self, nervous, and ill at ease. When asked *"What if..."* and *"Give me an example of a time when you..."* questions, has difficulty coming up with good responses that indicate an ability to produce outcomes and provide leadership. Intellectually curious but not good at closure. Appears somewhat academic: thinks a lot about issues but has difficulty in quickly drawing conclusions and taking action. Lacks decisiveness in making decisions – a real time killer when it comes time to participate in meetings and work in teams. Communicates uncertainty with such comments as *"I don't know," "Maybe," "I'm not sure," "Hadn't really thought of that," "Interesting question," "I'll have to think about that,"* or redirects with the question *"Well, what do you think?"* Not good leadership and team building material.

16. **Appears too eager and hungry for the job.** Is overly enthusiastic, engages in extreme flattery, gives self-centered answers to many interview questions, and appears suspiciously nervous. Early in the interview, before learning much about the company or job, makes such comments as *"I really like it here," "I really need this job," "Is there overtime?," "What are you paying?," "How many vacation days do you give?"* Something does not feel right about this candidate. The gut feeling is that this one is likely to be more trouble than he is worth!

17. **Communicates dishonesty or deception.** Uses canned interview language, evades probing questions, frequently changes the subject, and appears disingenuous. Looks like a tricky character who has things to hide and thus will probably be sneaky and deceptive on the job. When asked why he worked for three different employers during the past four years, says he had the misfortunate of being "laid off." Quickly changes the subject rather than give details on why he was chosen for the layoffs. Something is not right here.

18. **Demonstrates extreme role-playing to the point of being too smooth and superficial.** Dresses nicely, has a firm handshake and good eye contact, answers most questions okay, appears enthusiastic, and keeps repeating the same redundant 30-second elevator speech or storyline about his key strengths – just like some popular interview books and videos tell job seekers to do. But when asked more substantive *"What if"* and behavior-based questions, or requested to give examples of specific accomplishments, the candidate seems to be caught off balance and stumbles, giving incomplete answers or repeating that same 30-second storyline that question his ability to think on his feet or move outside the mental box he has put himself in. Can't put one's finger on the problem, but the gut reaction is that this role-playing candidate is very superficial and will probably end up being the "dressed for success" and "coached for the interview" employee from hell!

19. Appears evasive when asked about possible problems with background.
Gives evasive answers or tries to change the subject in reference to red flag questions about lack of skills and experience, limited education, frequent job changes, termination, and time gaps in work history. Such responses raise questions about the interviewee's honesty, credibility, responsibility, and overall behavior. Indicates a possible negative behavior pattern that probably needs further investigation.

20. Speaks negatively of previous employers and co-workers. When asked why she left previous employers, usually responds by bad-mouthing them. Has little good to say about others who apparently were not as important as this candidate. Does not appear to be a team player. Seems to be very self-centered and arrogant.

21. Maintains poor eye contact. Candidate has "shifty eyes" that raise suspicions about his truthfulness and forthrightness. While he may be shy, his vague answers to questions accompanied by irritating eye contact sends mixed verbal/nonverbal messages that disrupt the flow of the interview.

At least in America, eye contact is viewed as an indication of trustworthiness and attention. Individuals who fail to maintain an appropriate amount of eye contact are often judged as untrustworthy – have something to hide. Having too little or too much eye contact during the interview gives off mixed messages about what the candidate is saying. Worst of all, it may make the interviewer feel uncomfortable in the interviewee's presence.

22. Offers a limp or overly firm handshake. Interviewers often get two kinds of handshakes from candidates – the wimps and the bone-crushers. Your initial handshake may be viewed as saying something about your personality. Candidates offering a cold, wet, and limp handshake often come across as corpses! Bone-crushers may appear too aggressive.

23. Comes unprepared and shows little interest in the company. Indicates he didn't do much research, since he knows little about the company and didn't take time to check out the company's website. Asks this killer question: *"What do you do here?"* Few answers to questions relate to the interests of the company. Fails to ask questions that would indicate an interest in the job or the company.

24. Talks about salary and benefits early in the interview. Rather than try to learn more about the company and position as well as demonstrate her value (she does say she can easily do the job), the candidate seems preoccupied with salary and benefits by talking about them within the first 15 minutes of the interview. Shows little interest in the job or employer beyond the compensation package.

Interviewers read between the lines for red flags. When an interviewee prematurely talks about compensation, a big red flag goes up. Such a line of questioning usually indicates this is a self-centered candidate who is not really interested in doing the job. Their primary interest is salary and benefits.

25. **Is discourteous, ill-mannered, and disrespectful.** Arrives for the interview a half hour late with no explanation or a phone call indicating a problem en route. Just sits and waits for the interviewer to ask questions. Picks up things on the interviewer's desk. Challenges the interviewer's ideas. Closes the interview without thanking the interviewer for the opportunity to interview for the job. Not even going to charm and etiquette school would help this candidate!

26. **Appears socially awkward.** Seems to have difficulty meeting people, maintaining good eye contact, and sustaining even a short conversation. The clothes, shoes, and jewelry don't seem to fit right or come together well. Appears uncomfortable in the presence of others. Table manners and drinking behavior leave much to be desired.

27. **Tells inappropriate jokes and laughs a lot.** Attempts at humor bomb – appears to be a smart ass who likes to laugh at his own jokes. Comes across as an irritating clown who says stupid and silly things. Will need to isolate this one to keep him away from other employees who don't share such humor and tastelessness.

28. **Talks too much.** Can't answer a question without droning on and on with lots of irrelevant talk. Volunteers all kinds of information, including interesting but sensitive personal observations and gossip the interviewer neither needs nor wants. Doesn't know when to shut up. Would probably waste a lot of valuable work time talking, talking, and talking and thus irritating other employees. Seems to need lots of social strokes through talk, which she readily initiates.

29. **Argues with the interviewer.** Disagrees with interviewer about management philosophy, marketing approaches, new initiatives, and the job search. Appears to have a contentious personality that is likely to clash with other members of the team he'll be working with.

30. **Drops names to impress the interviewer.** Talks about all the important people he knows who are his "friends." Tells stories about how important he is to those people and how much they admire him, including his Facebook page. Unclear how such name-dropping relates to the job in question. Perhaps he thinks the interviewer will be impressed with a verbal Rolodex of who he knows.

But interviewers tend to be put off by such candidates who, instead, appear to be insecure, arrogant, and patronizing – three deadly sins that may shorten your interview from 45 minutes to 15 minutes! The truth about the extent of their "friendship" with such people is suspect. If they know the candidate well, why are they not included on the candidate's list of references?

31. **Appears needy and greedy.** Talks a lot about financial needs and compensation. When discussing salary, talks about his personal financial situation, including debts and planned future purchases, rather than what the job is worth and what value he will bring to the job. Seems to expect the employer is interested in supporting his lifestyle, which may be a combination of irresponsible financial behavior, failing to plan, living beyond his pay grade, and having bad luck. This line of talk indicates he probably has debilitating financial problems that go far beyond the salary level of this job. A background check may indicate financial difficulties.

32. **Closes the interview by just leaving.** When asked if she has any questions, says *"No"* and gets up and leaves after shaking hands and saying *"Thank you for meeting with me."*

    Most interviewees fail to properly close interviews. How you close the interview may determine whether or not you will be invited back to another interview or offered the job. Never ever end the interview with this stupid and presumptuous closing prior to being offered the job: *"So when can I start?"* This question will likely finish off the interview and your candidacy – you're back to being needy and greedy! Also, don't play the pressure game, even if it's true, by stating *"I have another interview this week. When can I expect to hear from you?"* One other critical element to this close: send a nice thank-you letter within 24 hours in which you again express your appreciation for the interview and your interest in the job.

33. **Fails to talk about accomplishments.** Candidate concentrates on explaining work history as primarily consisting of assigned duties and responsibilities. When asked to give examples of her three major accomplishments in her last jobs, doesn't seem to understand the question, gives little evidence of performance, or reverts once again to discussing formal duties and responsibilities. When probed further for accomplishments, doesn't really say much and shows discomfort about this line of questioning.

34. **Does not ask questions about the job or employer.** Seems to view the interview as a forum to which he has come to answer the interviewer's questions. When asked *"Do you have any questions?,"* the candidate replies *"No"* or *"You've covered everything."*

Asking questions is often more important to getting the job than answering questions. Your questions should focus on learning more about the position, job, and employer. When you ask thoughtful questions, you emphasize your interest in the employer and job as well as indicate your intelligence – qualities employers look for in candidates. Most important of all, you acquire critical information from which to decide whether or not you really want the job!

35. **Too effusive and self-effacing.** Appears nervous and overly anxious to please the interviewer by being extremely deferential and self-effacing. Has difficulty giving simple and straightforward answers to questions. Seems to lack self-confidence and thus appears compelled to go into unnecessary detail while answering questions. Doesn't know when it is appropriate to stop talking and move on to other more important matters. Such behaviors raise suspicions about the candidate – what's really beneath the surface?

36. **Appears self-centered rather than employer-centered.** Candidate appears to be preoccupied with himself, focusing on benefits he will receive rather than contributions he is likely to make to the organization. This orientation becomes immediately apparent by the direction of the answers and questions coming from the interviewee. It reveals a great deal about his motivations and possible work behavior. If the candidate primarily focuses on employee benefits, he will be perceived as **self-centered**. For example, a candidate who frequently uses "I" when talking about himself and the job may be very self-centered. On the other hand, the candidate who talks about "we" and "you" is usually more **employer-oriented**. Contrast these paired statements about the job and compensation:

"What would I be doing in this position?"

"What do you see us achieving over the next six months?"

or

"What would I be making on this job?"

"What do you normally pay for someone with my qualifications?"

37. **Demonstrates poor listening skills.** Doesn't listen carefully to questions or seems to have her own agenda that overrides the interviewer's interest. Tends to go off in different directions from the questions being asked. Not a very empathetic listener both verbally and nonverbally. Seems to be more interested in talking about own agenda than focusing on the issues at hand. Apparently wants to take charge of the interview and be the Lone Ranger. The job really does require good listening skills!

38. **Seems not bright enough for the job.** Answering simple interview questions is like taking an intelligence test. Candidate has difficulty talking about past accomplishments. Doesn't seem to grasp what the job is all about or the skills required. Seems confused and lacks focus. Should never have gotten to the job interview but had a terrific looking resume that was probably written by a professional resume writer!

39. **Fails to know his/her worth and negotiate properly when it comes time to talk about compensation.** Candidate talks about salary and benefits early the interview. When salary is discussed, he appears to be fine with the first figure offered.

     Job seekers are well advised to only talk about salary and benefits **after** being offered the job. If you prematurely talk about compensation, you may diminish your value as well as appear self-centered. Be sure to research salary comparables so you know what you are worth in today's job market (start with www. salary. com). Listen carefully throughout the interview and ask questions that would give you a better idea of what the job is actually worth. Stress throughout the interview your skills and accomplishments – those things that are most valued by employers who are willing to pay what's necessary for top talent. When you do start negotiating, let the **employer** state a salary figure first and then negotiate using salary ranges to reach common ground.

40. **Fails to properly prepare for the interview.** This is the most important mistake of all. It affects all the other mistakes. Indeed, failing to prepare will immediately show when the candidate makes a bad first impression, fails to indicate knowledge about the company and job, fails to give good answers to standard interview questions, does not ask thoughtful questions, prematurely talks about salary and benefits, and leaves the interview without closing properly. In other words, the candidate makes many of the mistakes outlined above because he or she failed to anticipate what goes into a winning interview.

Interview Tips From the Experts

Numerous online and print resources can help you avoid many of the mistakes outlined in this chapter. If you need help in preparing for the job interview, we recommend searching for job interview segments on YouTube.com. Use any combination of the following **keywords** in searching the YouTube website:

- job interview
- job interview questions and answers
- job interview tips
- job interview examples
- interview mistakes

The following **books** also offer a wealth of tips on improving your job interview skills:

101 Dynamite Questions to Ask at Your Job Interview
101 Great Answers to the Toughest Interview Questions
250 Job Interview Questions You'll Most Likely Be Asked
301 Smart Answers to Tough Interview Questions
Art of the Interview
Best Answers to 202 Job Interview Questions
Boost Your Interview I.Q.
Don't Blow the Interview
How to Ace the Brain Teaser Interview
How to Answer Interview Questions
I Can't Believe They Asked Me That!
Interview Magic
Interview Power
Interview Rehearsal Book
Job Interview Tips for People With Not-So-Hot Backgrounds
Job Interviews for Dummies
KeyWords to Nail Your Job Interview
Knock 'Em Dead Job Interview
Nail the Job Interview!
Naked at the Interview
Perfect Phrases for the Perfect Interview
Power Interviews
Savvy Interviewing
Win the Interview, Win the Job
Winning the Interview Game
Winning Job Interview
You Should Hire Me!
You've Got the Interview

Hundreds of career and job search **websites** offer great interview tips. Many also include video clips of mock job interviews. Use the same five keywords on the previous page that I recommended for YouTube.com when searching for job interview tips and examples on various search engines. Also, search for **"job interview apps"** which will generate a variety of useful apps for smart phones, from maps and calendars to sample Q&As and tips on dressing and tying a tie! Get started by visiting the following websites:

- **Monster**   www.monster.com/career-advice/job-interview
- **The Balance**   www.thebalance.com/job-interview-questions-and-answers-2061204

- **Job Hunt**   www.job-hunt.org/job_interviews/job-interviewing.shtml
- **The Muse**   www.themuse.com/advice/how-to-answer-the-31-most-common-interview-questions
- **Job Interview**   www.job-interview.net
- **Live Career**   www.livecareer.com/quintessential/job-interview-tips

6

The Verbal Exchange of Questions and Answers

---

*"Effective interviewees communicate their **strengths** to employers who have very specific hiring **needs**. Employers don't just hire for the fun of it. They have **positions** to fill and **jobs** to get done."*

THE KEY WORDS IN THIS CHAPTER are "prepare" and "employer's needs." **Preparation** is necessary for putting your honest and best self forward in the interview. This is true for any job applicant, but especially so anyone with red flags in his background. What you say and do during the interview may well overcome any deficiencies in your background. Your goal is to make the employer feel confident that he or she is making the right hiring decision. Throughout the interview you must be **employer-centered** rather than self-centered. If you can focus as such, you'll be well on your way to acing the job interview!

Meeting the employer's needs means that you should try to determine what the company's needs are and how you could fill them, rather than view the interview only from your own perspective of needs and wants. Remember, the interview is not all about you – it's primarily about meeting the employer's needs. During every step of the interview process, you need to remain **focused** on what's really important. Do that by repeating this **reality check question** – *"Am I clearly communicating how I will meet the employer's needs?"*

Gather Information About the Company and the Job

Find out as much about the company as you can. Search for information about the company on the Internet. Today, most companies, even small businesses, have an Internet presence – either a dedicated website or Facebook page. Although many of these sites serve primarily as advertisements for the company's goods or services, this information can be useful to you as you prepare for an interview. Large corporations often have an "employment" section on their website that lists positions they are trying to fill. Many company websites provide a wealth of information on operations, including profiles of key personnel (perhaps there is information on the person who will be conducting your job interview) and helpful hints on applying for a job. Check out this website for candid reviews of companies by their employees, who share insider information on what it's like working in various companies, including the good, bad, and ugly: www.glassdoor.com.

Do you know people who work at the company or have worked there in the past? Talk to them about what the company does, what it is like to work there, what kind of jobs they offer. Ask as many specific questions as you can think of. For example, when asking what it is like to work there, what do you really want to know? What are the normal working hours? What is the opportunity for overtime? What is the likelihood you will be asked to take any tests during the interview stage? How many paid holidays there are? Sick leave? Vacation days? What other benefits does the company offer?

Ask questions about day-to-day working for the company as well. What is/was the person's boss like? Are the employees' concerns listened to and taken into account? Has the company been facing any problems lately – with sales, product line, competition from other firms? Are they up-to-date on technology or are they operating in the Stone Age? Your data gathering questions generally cover five categories:

- questions about what you might expect at a job interview
- questions about benefits
- questions about what it is like to work there
- questions about problems the company may face
- questions about opportunities to learn and grow at the company

If you know what the job opening is, ask questions about the particular job you are applying for. This is the time you can ask questions about your own self-interests. Once you are in the job interview, questions concerning job benefits should **not** be asked until the end of the interview, and many job search authorities would advise you not to ask these self-centered benefit questions until you have been offered the job. Remember, throughout the job interview your focus should be on meeting the **employer's** needs. You should be constantly presenting a picture of a **competent problem solver**.

You can find a wealth of information on companies – especially large or publicly held companies – which are readily accessible at your local library and online. Ask the librarian to help you locate materials that are available. Ex-offenders quickly discover that local libraries are one of their best friends for accessing important re-entry resources.

Match Your Goals/Strengths to the Employer's Needs

The more you know about the job opening and how the job fits into the company's overall product line or service offerings, the better you can determine your **"fit"** – how your skills and experience will meet with the employer's needs. Prepare to be able to talk about this "fit" during the interview. Practice the **"gist"** of what you might say in a minute or two to convince the employer of how your skills/experience meet the company's needs.

Don't try to memorize this – just be familiar with the main points you want to make. And don't worry if the way you say it in the actual interview is not exactly the way you said it when you prepared for or practiced for the interview. That's the whole idea of having in mind the "gist" of what you want to say. The "gist" is your strategy. It is the basic idea(s) you want to convey. Say it in the way that comes naturally to you each time you want to communicate that idea. The actual words will probably be somewhat different each time.

Prepare to Complete an Application

For many jobs, if you have a resume you will not be asked to fill out a job application. Other employers will require you to complete an online or paper application whether or not you have a resume. Not only does the completed application provide necessary information to the employer, but how you fill it out speaks volumes as well. It's primarily designed to screen your "in" or "out" for formal face-to-face job interviews. As you complete an application, ask yourself:

- Did I understand the questions?
- Did I fill out the application completely, or did I leave some spaces blank?
- Did I fill out the application neatly, or did I cross out some things?
- What about spelling and grammar – are they correct?

How well did I respond to sensitive questions, such as *"Have you ever been convicted of a felony? If yes, explain."* (Despite the growing "ban the box" movement, many employers still ask this question on application forms)

In other words, the application you complete in the employer's office tells the employer a lot more than you might think.

Before you leave home for the interview, anticipate the kinds or questions you may be asked to complete on an application form. Some of the likely questions include:

- Education completed and relevant dates
- Former jobs held, including the name of the company and its address and phone number, relevant dates, and the name of your immediate supervisor
- Dates served in the military (if applicable), date of discharge, type of discharge
- Names and contact information for references

Be sure you know you Social Security number since many employers will ask for it. These things are the minimum information you should take with you to the job interview. You may think of other things that are pertinent to your job situation, such as on-the-job training or courses you completed while employed elsewhere.

Organize Your References

Consider carefully the people you will use as references. The strongest references from the employer's viewpoint will come from individuals in the business community – ideally individuals who have some familiarity with the work you do even though you may not have worked for them or have done so in a non-traditional way. For example, if you mowed lawns for a prominent business person when you were younger and impressed that individual with your energy and drive or perhaps your attention to detail, that person could be a good reference even though you did not work in their company. If you have had a job while you were incarcerated and demonstrated positive work habits, your supervisor on that job could be a good person to ask to serve as a reference. Remember you are not trying to hide the fact that you have spent time in prison. Rather, you want to show that you have made positive changes in your life and have turned your life around.

Once you have determined who your strongest references will be, ask their permission to use them as a reference. This is considered the proper way to deal with personal references, and it will further impress upon the individual whose support you want that you are a conscientious person who does things properly. This contact with the potential reference serves other purposes as well. It gives the individual a chance to decline your request if he feels he doesn't know you well enough or cannot give you a good recommendation. It also provides an opportunity for you to review your strengths which you hope your reference will mention on your behalf.

If this person is aware of red flags you have in your past, it gives you the opportunity to remind your potential reference how you have changed your situation and overcame, or are working on overcoming, your past problems.

Take all the contact information on your references – names (correctly spelled), title (if applicable), addresses, emails, and phone numbers – with you to the job interview so you can accurately fill out an application if you are asked to complete one. Remember to also take information about your education, past jobs, military service, and any specialized training you may have received with you to the interview in order to complete questions about these areas accurately on an application. You goal is to complete the application as thoroughly, accurately, and quickly as possible. Providing incomplete information communicates bad messages – you're unprepared or hiding something!

Prepare for Questions

You will be asked many questions during the job interview. For example, you may be asked questions related to their general categories:

- questions about your personal life
- questions about your education
- questions about your experience

- questions about your skill levels and competencies
- questions about your failures/weaknesses
- questions about your accomplishments
- questions about what motivates you
- questions about your future goals/plans
- questions about your ability to solve problems
- questions about handling stress
- questions about your rehabilitation

Again, it is important that you prepare for the questions you are most likely to face. Yes, it will take time to prepare to succeed. But if it isn't worth the effort to prepare to succeed in the interview, why waste your time going to the interview at all?

You can anticipate most of the questions you are likely to be asked. Sit down and make a list of those questions you can expect to be asked, and don't forget to include questions about any red flags in your past. You generated a list of red flags in Chapter 4. Use the following general list to divide questions into categories.

- **Questions I am likely to be asked in an interview:**

  _____

  _____

  _____

  _____

- **Questions about my personal life:**

  _____

  _____

  _____

  _____

- **Questions about my education:**

  _____

  _____

  _____

  _____

- **Questions about my skill levels and competencies:**

  _____
  _____
  _____
  _____

- **Questions about my work experience:**

  _____
  _____
  _____
  _____

- **Questions about my accomplishments:**

  _____
  _____
  _____
  _____

- **Questions about my failures/weaknesses:**

  _____
  _____
  _____
  _____

- **Questions about what motivates me:**

  _____
  _____
  _____
  _____

- **Questions about my future goals/plans:**

  _____
  _____
  _____
  _____

- **Questions about my ability to solve problems:**

  _____

  _____

  _____

  _____

- **Questions about handling stress:**

  _____

  _____

  _____

  _____

- **Questions about my rehabilitation:**

  _____

  _____

  _____

  _____

You have listed many questions you believe an employer might ask you during a job interview. No, you probably won't be asked all of these questions, but you will no doubt encounter many of them. How will you respond? Do you have well thought-out answers? For example, how would you respond to a question about what motivates you or about your future plans and goals? Have you thought about this aspect of your life? Now is a far better time to consider your answers to questions like these than when they come up in the middle of your job interview!

Go back through the questions you have listed above (either by yourself or with a partner) and formulate the "gist" of how you would respond. As always when strategizing your "gist" responses, don't try to memorize a response. Think in terms of framing an answer that is both honest and positive at the same time. In politics this is called putting a positive "spin" on a situation.

101 Frequently Asked Job Interview Questions

Career experts and job seeker report that the following questions are frequently asked by interviewers and they prepare accordingly. In fact, you may have already identified several of the questions in the previous section. Indeed, you should be able to predict 95 percent of the questions that are likely to be asked in most interviews. Added to the questions you generated on pages 55-57, use the following pages as a handy checklist to prepare for your next interview.

As you plan responses to each question, again remember to formulate a **strategy**. You should not try to formulate the exact words you would use and then memorize them. To do this would be a big mistake. At best your answer would likely sound memorized and you would greatly diminish your credibility. At worst, you might forget your memorized response in the middle of your answer because you are so nervous!

So consider your answers in terms of basic strategies. What do you hope to convey as you respond to each question? Your goal is to convince the interviewer that you should be offered the job. As you get ready to respond, think in terms of the needs of the employer. How do your goals fit with her business needs? Keep this basic tenet in mind as you formulate your strategies in response to questions you are asked. Try to make time prior to the interview to actually talk through your answers to questions. You may practice answering interview questions (which you have made into a list) posed by a friend or family member or you can read each question and then respond. Practice talking your answers into a recording device. Play back the recording and evaluate how you sound:

- Do you exude confidence?
- Do you sound dynamic?
- Do you talk in a conversational style? (rather than your response sounding like a "canned" memorized answer)
- Do you speak without excessive fillers such as *"ah," "and ah," "like,"* and *"you know"*?
- Do you seem believable and trustworthy?
- Do you appear likable?

Each time you talk through an answer, your words will be somewhat different since you have purposely not tried to memorize your response. You have thought through the strategy of your response, the "gist" of the message you want to convey, but you have not attempted to commit a response to memory.

Personality and Motivation

1. Why should we hire you?_____

   _____

2. Are you a self-starter?_____

   _____

3. What is your greatest strength?_____

   _____

4. What is your greatest weakness?_____

_____

5. What would you most like to improve about yourself? _____

_____

6. What are some of the reasons for your success? _____

_____

7. Describe your typical workday._____

_____

8. Do you anticipate problems or do you react to them?_____

_____

9. How do you deal with stressful situations? _____

_____

10. Do you ever lose your temper?_____

_____

11. How well do you work under deadlines?_____

_____

12. What contributions did you make to your last (or present) company?_____

_____

13. What will you bring to this position that others won't? _____

_____

14. How well do you get along with your superiors?_____

_____

15. How well do you get along with your co-workers? _____

_____

16. How do you manage your subordinates? _____

_____

17. How do you feel about working with superiors who may be less educated or younger than you? _____

_____

18. Do you prefer working alone or with others? _____

_____

19. How do others view your work? _____

_____

20. How do you deal with criticism? _____

_____

21. Do you consider yourself to be someone who takes greater initiative than others?

_____

22. Do you consider yourself a risk-taker? _____

_____

23. Are you a good time manager? _____

_____

24. How important is job security? _____

_____

25. How do you define success? _____

_____

26. How do you spend your leisure time? _____

_____

27. What would be the perfect job for you? _____

_____

28. What really motivates you to perform on the job? _____

_____

29. How old are you? _____

_____

30. What does your spouse or significant other think about your career? _____

_____

31. Are you living with anyone? _____

_____

32. Do you have many debts? _____

_____

33. Do you own or rent your home? _____

_____

34. What social or political organizations do you belong to? _____

_____

Education and Training

35. Why didn't you go to college? _____

_____

36. Why didn't you finish high school or college? _____

_____

37. Why did you select _____ college? _____

_____

38. Why did you major in _____ ? _____

_____

39. What was your minor in school? _____

_____

40. How did your major relate to the work you have done since graduation? _____

_____

41. Why weren't your grades better in school? _____

_____

42. What subjects did you enjoy most? _____

_____

43. What subjects did you enjoy least? _____
_____

44. If you could go back and do it over again, what would you change about your
education? _____
_____

45. What extracurricular activities did you participate in at school/college? _____
_____

46. Tell me about your role in (<u>one of your extracurricular activities</u>). _____
_____

47. What leadership positions did you hold in school? _____
_____

48. How does your diploma/degree/certificate prepare you for the job at ? _____
_____

49. Did you work part-time or full-time while you were in college? _____
_____

50. Are you planning to take additional courses over the next year or two? _____
_____

51. If you had a choice of several short training sessions to attend, which two or three
would you select? _____
_____

52. What materials do you read regularly to keep up with what is going on in your field?
_____

53. What is the most recent skill you have learned? What additional skills would you
like to learn? _____
_____

54. What are your educational goals over the next few years? _____
_____

Experience and Skills

55. Why do you want to leave your present job or previous jobs?_____
_____

56. Why have you changed jobs so frequently? _____
_____

57. Why would you be more likely to stay here? _____
_____

58. What are your qualifications for this job?_____
_____

59. What experience prepares you for this job? _____
_____

60. What did you like most about your present/most recent job?_____
_____

61. What did you like least about that job?_____
_____

62. What did you like most about your boss?_____
_____

63. What did you like least about that boss?_____
_____

64. Tell me about an ongoing responsibility in your current/most recent job that you enjoyed. _____
_____

65. How does your present job (or most recent) relate to the overall goals of your department/the company?_____
_____

66. What has your present/most recent supervisor(s) criticized about your work? ____
_____

67. What duties in your present/most recent job do you find it difficult to do? _____

_____

68. Why do you want to leave your present job? Are you being forced out?_____

_____

69. Why should we hire someone like you – with your experience and motivation?

_____

70. What type of person would you hire for this position?_____

_____

71. Have you ever been fired or asked to resign? _____

_____

72. What was the most important contribution you made on your last job? _____

_____

73. What do you wish you had accomplished in your present/most recent job but
were unable to? _____

_____

74. What is the most important thing you've learned from the jobs you've held?____

_____

Career Goals

75. Tell me about yourself. _____

_____

76. Tell me about your career goals._____

_____

77. What would you like to accomplish during the next five years (or ten years).

_____

78. How do your career goals today differ from your career goals five years ago?

_____

79. Where do you see yourself five years from now?_____

_____

80. Describe a major goal you set for yourself recently? _____

_____

81. What are you doing to achieve that goal?_____

_____

82. Have you ever thought of switching careers?_____

_____

83. How does this job compare to what would be the perfect job for you? _____

_____

84. What would you change about our company to make this your ideal workplace?

_____

85. How long have you been looking for a job?_____

_____

Why You Want This Job

86. What do you know about our company? _____

_____

87. What trends do you see in our industry?_____

_____

88. Why do you want to work for us?_____

_____

89. How much business would you bring to our firm?_____

_____

90. What similarities do you see between this and your current/most recent position?

_____

91. What makes this position different from your current/most recent position?

_____

92. Why are you willing to take a job you are over-qualified for? _____

_____

93. Why are you willing to take a pay cut from your previous (or present) position?

_____

94. What would you change about this position? _____

_____

95. How long would you expect to stay with our company? _____

_____

96. How do you feel about working overtime or on weekends?_____

_____

97. Are you willing to relocate? _____

_____

98. How much are you willing to travel? _____

_____

99. What are your salary expectations?_____

_____

100. How soon could you begin work?_____

_____

101. Do you have any questions? _____

_____

Unexpected Questions

You may not be asked any questions beyond the ones outlined above. If the questions you are asked do go beyond these, they will most likely fall into one of two categories:

- Specific questions that relate to special knowledge or skills required for the job for which you are being considered.

- Questions that are raised by unusual items or unexplained gaps or omissions on your resume or application.

Look over your resume and/or application for anticipating additional questions. Is there anything that stands out? Do you see patterns that might raise questions? If you spent the last three years in prison but indicate under "Experience" that you worked for the State of Wisconsin, which you honestly did, the interviewer may want to probe the type of state job you held. If you have a two- to five-year unexplained gap in your work history, this gap is bound to raise the question of what you were doing during this time. You need to be ready with honest, yet positive answers, that will further promote your candidacy rather than knock you out of the running.

If you have thoughtfully considered your responses and practiced responding with the "gist" of the message you want to convey, these questions should not throw you. However, if you haven't given such questions much thought, your responses are likely to show it.

Few questions should ever be answered with just a *"yes"* or *"no."* Remember to provide **examples** as often as possible to **illustrate or support** the points you make. If asked by the interviewer whether you are a self-starter, you could simply respond *"yes."* However, you score few points for this response. It really says nothing except that either you think you are a self-starter, or you think this is the response the interviewer wants to hear. But if you follow your *"yes"* response with an example or two of what you did that demonstrates you were a self-starter in your last, you start to sell yourself. You want to impress the interviewer and you want to stand out from the rest of the applicants being interviewed.

Remember to **use examples** and use them frequently. Examples support assertions about your abilities and thus help sell you to the interviewer. Examples make what you say about your skills and achievements more clear, more interesting, more credible, and more likely to be remembered. They help tell your **story**.

Behavior- and Situation-Based Questions

Employers increasingly incorporate behavior-based and situation-based questions in job interviews. "Behavior-based" means that the interviewer asks you to describe how you responded when faced with an actual situation. "Hypothetical situational-based" questions don't ask for an actual situation; they ask you to imagine a situation and describe how you would act if that occurred. Interviewers often refer to these as *"What if..."* questions. These types of questions attempt to get applicants to do what they should be doing anyway: expanding their answers with examples that support the assertions they are making. Such questions require you to literally "think on your feet" in communicating your competencies. When asking these types of questions, interviews look for tell-tale signs of strengths and weaknesses in interviewees.

Be prepared to respond to these types of open-ended behavior-based and situation-based questions:

1. What would you do if . . . ? _____

_____

2. In what situations have you become so involved in the work you were doing that the day flew by?_____

_____

3. If you were to encounter that same situation now, how would you deal with that person?_____

_____

4. If you had a choice of working in our department A or department B, which would you choose? _____

_____

5. Why would you make that choice? _____

_____

6. Tell me about a recent time when you took responsibility for a task that was outside of our job description._____

_____

7. Tell me about a time when you took action without your supervisor's prior approval.

_____

Be prepared to give lots of real-life examples about your judgment and performance when answering these challenging types of questions.

7

Nonverbal Behaviors to Win the Job Interview

"What you say nonverbally in the interview carries more weight than the verbal content of your answers. Neglect your nonverbal communication and you may be dead upon arrival. Indeed, don't be surprised if the interview ends quickly!"

WHAT YOU SAY VERBALLY DURING the interview relays a lot of information about you, the job applicant, to the interviewer. You are also communicating information nonverbally. Because it is more difficult to control our nonverbal behavior, it is more difficult for us to intentionally manipulate and convey false messages. Thus, nonverbal messages are thought to be more honest and revealing than verbal ones.

Manage Your Physical Appearance and Dress – Men

The first thing the interviewer will notice is your physical appearance and the way you dress. Take, for example, the group photo on the front cover of this book. What does it imply about the people, especially their competency and likability? Would you want to interview any of them? Which ones?

Before you open your mouth to speak, the employer is already making judgments about you. These judgments concern your competence, whether you are trustworthy, whether you would be a good "fit" in the organization. How can he determine these things just by looking at you? He can't. But he makes judgments and comes to conclusions about you just the same, because he needs to quickly simplify his choices. We all do it. You have done it too – about your teachers in school, potential employers, people you encountered in prison, and people you meet on the street. Whether it is fair or not, it is reality. Know that the interviewer is sizing you up as soon as he sees you. Make this fact of life work for you by planning and managing your appearance and dress to put you in the best light possible. Make your appearance convey positive things about you.

If, for example, you have a case of adult ADHD (Attention Deficit Hyperactivity Disorder), you may appear rude and disinterested in the job as your mind tends to wander during the interview. Consequently, your apparent lack of focus and concentration would leave a bad impression on the employer.

Make certain you are clean and neatly groomed from head to toe. You are freshly showered, including clean and neat hair. You smell good, but your scent is not overpowering. You have applied deodorant (this is a "must") and perhaps a light cologne (optional). If you use a scent, do not apply it with a heavy hand. A strong scent can be a real turn-off and work against you. If hired, you will be working with these people daily. The negatives of body odor or an overpowering cologne could be enough to lose you the job opportunity. Your fingernails are trimmed and clean. Your teeth are freshly brushed and you have used mouthwash. You should be freshly shaven.

If you're heavily tattooed, try to minimize the "show" with appropriate clothing. While you may have an interesting story to tell, you don't want the interview to focus on your tattoo history and judgment – where, when, and why. Indeed, there's a high probability your story will not produce a good post-interview outcome!

Your clothing should be clean, neat, and relatively conservative. This is not the time to emulate the dress of your favorite rock star or rap artist. The most dressed down attire for a man is a freshly laundered and pressed (or a fabric that looks pressed) shirt and clean pair of slacks. Wear socks, even if it isn't "cool," and polished shoes. This clean and neat but dressed down attire would be appropriate if you are applying for a job stocking shelves, working in an auto-repair facility, or a similar type of job.

If you are applying for a job other than in a "blue collar" field, dress the outfit up a bit by adding a sport jacket and necktie. Of course, for a white collar job, a suit and tie would be most appropriate. You can always dress up to the next higher level than the job you are applying for as long as you feel comfortable. This would be an example of exceeding the employer's expectations.

Manage Your Physical Appearance and Dress – Women

The first thing the interviewer will notice is your physical appearance and the way you dress. Before you open your mouth to speak, the employer is already making judgments about you. These judgments concern your competence, whether you are trustworthy, whether you would be a good "fit" in the organization. How can he determine these things just by looking at you? He can't. But he makes judgments and comes to conclusions about you just the same. We all do it. You have done it too – about your teachers in school, potential employers, and people you meet on the street. Whether it is fair or not, it is reality. Know that the interviewer is sizing you up as soon as he sees you. Make this fact of life work for you by planning and managing your appearance and dress to put you in the best light possible. Make your appearance convey positive things about you.

Make certain you are clean and neat from head to toe. You are freshly showered and your hair is clean and neatly styled. You smell good. You have applied deodorant (a "must") and if you wish to use a light cologne (optional) you have applied it sparingly.

Body odor or a too strong scent can be a real turn-off and work against you. Your fingernails are trimmed and clean. If you use polish, a natural shade is best. A light pink might be acceptable, but, please, no "funky" colors such as purple or green. Your teeth are freshly brushed and you have used mouthwash.

Your clothing should be clean, neat, and relatively conservative. The most dressed down attire for a woman is a freshly laundered and pressed blouse and a clean pair of slacks. Wear polished shoes, flats or a low heel, that match or are darker than the color of the slacks. This is not the time to wear that new pair of clunky clogs or stiletto heels. Shoes that are lighter in color than your slacks will call attention to your feet; you want the interviewer to concentrate on your face. Nylons in a skin tone will best complement your look. This clean and neat but informal attire would be appropriate if you are applying for a job stocking shelves, waitressing, or similar position. If you are applying for most other jobs, or any job where you would have face-to-face contact with customers, dress up a notch. Wear slacks or a skirt and a matching blazer-type jacket or wear a top that matches your slacks or skirt and add a contrasting blazer or one that is a plaid with one of the colors in the plaid matching the color of your slacks and top. Low-heeled shoes that match or are as dark or darker than your slacks or skirt will look best. If applying for a professional position, your best bet is a skirted suit.

Getting Clothing Help

If you are relatively destitute and do not have the proper clothes for the job interview, check with various community organizations that help individuals with clothing, such as Goodwill Industries and the Salvation Army. You might also check out various local organizations that assist disadvantaged groups in dressing properly for job interviews, especially churches and welfare organizations. Many provide free attire for the asking. Here are a few such organizations that specialize in job search attire.

Attitudes and Attire (Dallas)	www.attitudesandattire.org
Bridge to Success (Chicago, IL)	www.thebridgetosuccess.org
Career Gear (8 communities – New York City, Baltimore, Washington DC, Houston, Hudson County, Miami, New Haven, San Antonio)	www.careergear.org
Clothes the Deal (Los Angeles)	www.clothesthedeal.org
Dress for Success (125 locations worldwide)	www.dressforsuccess.org
Jackets for Jobs, Inc. (Detroit)	www.jacketsforjobs.org
Suited for Change (Washington, DC)	www.suitedforchange.org
Wardrobe for Opportunity (Oakland, CA)	www.wardrobe.org

Many of these groups also provide a variety of job search training and mentoring services to ex-offenders, including tips on interviewing with local employers.

Make Your Body Language Say Positive Things About You

When you first meet the interviewer, your handshake should be firm and strong, but not so strong that you crush the employer's fingers in your grip. Avoid giving a limp handshake. The interviewer will probably indicate with a gesture where you are to sit. Once seated, don't slouch but, rather, sit erect and even with a very slight forward lean to the upper part of your body. To slouch in your chair conveys a detachment from the situation that suggests this interview isn't really very important to you, you are not interested in what is going on, or even that you are not too bright! To sit erect indicates you are alert, and the slight forward lean into the conversation conveys interest in the proceedings.

> *Sit erect and with a very slight forward lean.*

No slumped shoulders either. Slumped shoulders suggest that the weight of the world is on your shoulders and you are nearly beaten down. Who wants to hire a beaten down person? No squirming uncomfortably in the chair either. That is distracting to the interviewer, and may even suggest you have something to hide. Try not to fidget with your hands and avoid gestures with closed fists. Fidgeting behavior suggests you are nervous – who wouldn't be in a job interview – and have something to hide. Closed fists may convey aggressiveness.

So what positive signals can you convey through your body language?

DO:

- Sit fairly erect in the chair. This suggests you are alert, interested, and involved.
- Sit with a very slight forward lean to the upper part of your body. This conveys your interest in the conversation and the interviewer.
- Keep your hands open and relaxed so you can gesture when appropriate.
- Avoid clenching your hands together as you are less likely to use them to gesture.
- Avoid clenched fists which may suggest aggressive behavior.

DON'T:

- Fidget with your hands.
- Squirm (reposition yourself frequently) in the chair.

Gesture frequently if it is natural. Gestures help convey your interest and enthusiasm and help keep the interviewer's attention focused on your message as well.

Eye Contact and Facial Expression

Make frequent, although not constant, eye contact with the interviewer. The applicant who won't look the employer in the eye may be considered uninterested or even dishonest and hiding something. When we say, *"He couldn't look me in the eye,"* we suggest the person had something to hide. "Shifty eyes" is another term used to suggest a person may be less than honest. Look at the employer most of the time, looking away occasionally so neither of you feel uncomfortable.

Your facial expression should indicate your interest and enthusiasm.

By your facial expression you can indicate your interest and enthusiasm. A positive facial expression does not have to include a smile, but often will. A pleasant look on your face indicating interest is fine. Break into a smile occasionally when it seems appropriate. A smile adds life to most faces, and that life will be perceived as enthusiasm by the interviewer.

Avoid a face that appears angry (a scowl) or a stone face (no expression at all). Obviously, a face that appears angry will not convey positives to the employer, and a face devoid of expression will be interpreted negatively. You will be perceived as lacking interest in the job, the company, and the interviewer.

Vocal Expression

The final way you communicate nonverbally is by your tone of voice. Does your voice have vocal variety that conveys your interest and enthusiasm? Or does a lack of vocal variety (perhaps approaching a monotone) convey a lack of interest or enthusiasm?

Your Total Nonverbal Message

A combination of all the elements of nonverbal messages, taken together, can help or hinder you in the job interview. The way you manage your appearance and dress for the interview communicates to the employer whether you cared enough about the interview to clean up and dress appropriately. A slovenly appearance or inappropriate clothing suggests that you either don't know any better, or don't care.

Your body language – eye contact, facial expression, and your vocal expressiveness – further conveys your interest or lack of interest throughout the interview. If all the aspects of your nonverbal behavior are congruent – that is, they communicate the same message and that message is the same as your verbal message – then you will communicate a strong message to the interviewer that should be believable. If some of the aspects of your message are at odds with other aspects (for example, you say [verbally] you are interested in the job,

You should communicate similar verbal and nonverbal messages. If not, you will confuse the employer.

but your nonverbal messages suggest otherwise and contradict the verbal), the employer is likely to be confused. You say one thing, but act another. In this case the employer is likely to be uncomfortable with you for the job, and you will probably lose out on the chance at being hired.

So get your act together and communicate similar messages through your nonverbal behavior as you do with the words you say. Practice responding to expected questions in front of a mirror. What do you see? Is it an interested, enthusiastic job applicant?

Ask Yourself

1. **Why is the job applicant's appearance important for the job interview?**

   _____

   _____

   _____

   _____

2. **Why do people believe nonverbal messages are more truthful than verbal messages?**

   _____

   _____

   _____

   _____

3. **Name at least three ways you can nonverbally communicate to an interviewer that you are interested in the job you are applying for?**

   _____

   _____

   _____

   _____

8

Get Ready for the Interview

"If you're not prepared for one of the most important meetings of your life, then don't complain if you're passed over for the job. Take responsibility by preparing well for the critical job interview."

GETTING READY FOR THE critical job interview is all about preparation. Indeed, the watchwords for any job applicant should be preparation, preparation, preparation. You simply must put your best foot forward in the job interview if you want any change of getting a job offer.

Good Preparation Wins

Preparation takes time and effort, but if winning the job is important to you, it will be time well spent. If you decide to go to the interview and "wing it" – you don't take time to prepare because you are busy, lazy, or think you are so glib you can just talk a lot and fool the interviewer – think again. Chances are the employer has met job candidates like you before, and he will neither be impressed nor fooled. Employers are not stupid. Indeed, most are well prepared for you!

So do your homework. Put in the necessary time to go through the preparation for the job interview discussed in the previous chapters. It is no guarantee you will be offered every job you apply for, but preparation will give you a huge advantage over people with backgrounds similar to yours who do not take the time to prepare!

Most of Your Hard Work is Done!

You have been doing a lot of work as you went through the previous chapters. The activities you have completed provide information about you and your background. The strategies you have developed should provide the "gist" of your responses to most of the questions you are likely to be asked. As you do the final preparation for a job interview, this is a good time to go back and review the "gist" strategies you have developed and to add polish to any you wish to modify.

By now you should have formulated:

- A list of the most probable questions you may be asked in a job interview about: your personal life, your education, your work experience, your accomplishments, what motivates you as well as your future goals and plans – and the "gist" of your responses to them.

- A list of what you believe are your most positive workplace personality traits and real life examples of these traits from your life.

- The red flag behaviors in your past and the "gist" of how you will try to ease any concerns the employer may have about hiring you because of these red flag behaviors.

Go back over the information you have generated – especially the "gist" of your responses in these areas. Remember, you are not trying to memorize the information. This review is just to jog your thinking about the "gist" of what you think your response or any information you may want to volunteer should be.

A Word of Caution

You may recall the earlier suggestion that you want to be honest, but not stupid, as you take part in the job interview. What this means is that you should keep your comments about your past negative red flag behaviors focused and to the point. Be careful not to ramble on and on as you tell the whole ugly truth. A job interview is not a confessional! You do not need to dwell on this past behavior. Make the points we have suggested previously: take responsibility, indicate how your situation has changed, and your commitment to never again repeat the negative behavior. Make these points concisely. There is usually no need to elaborate a great deal on the negative behavior. Any elaboration should be on the positives – on how you have turned your life around. If the employer wants to know more about the offending behavior, he can ask. If this happens, try to make your response honest yet positive, and make it focused, short, and to the point.

You want to be honest, but not stupid. Admit your past red flags but focus on your positive changes and the future.

Last Minute Advice

Get a good night's sleep the night before your interview. You will feel better, look better, and be able to think more clearly to answer and ask questions of the interviewer if you are well rested.

Arrive at the interview site a bit earlier than the time set for the interview. Do a practice run a day or two before the interview if you are unsure of the location or how long it will take to get there. If you are driving, check ahead to find out what parking is available. Check whether you will have any time-consuming procedures upon arrival such as getting through a security check.

If you arrive early, you will have time to gather your thoughts rather than worry about whether you will be late. An early arrival will give you time to visit the restroom – you may need it if you feel nervous. You can re-check your appearance in the mirror as well.

Employers indicate the impression made by an applicant during the first 4-5 minutes of the job interview is seldom changed during the remainder of the interview, even if the interview lasts a half hour or more. You cannot make a very good impression on he interviewer during the first 4-5 minutes if you are not even there! If the job interview is not important enough to you that you can be prompt, the employer will have serious questions about he likelihood that you will have a good record of being on time if you were to get the job.

Go alone to the interview. Do not come with a friend, parent, or child.

Go alone to the interview. No friends nor children should accompany you. If you are dependent on a friend to drive you to he interview, have your friend drop you outside and meet you later rather than accompany you inside to the interview. Make sure though, that you will be able to get to work each day if you are offered and accept the job.

9

At the Interview:
Wow the Interviewer

"How well you perform in the interview session will determine whether or not you get the job offer. Everything you've done thus far to get the job rests on this critical face-to-face meeting."

THE JOB INTERVIEW IS ALL about making good impressions on **strangers** by how you look, what you say, and what you do before, during, and after the interview. Assuming you've arrived on time – a little early is even better – now it's time you shined throughout the interview, from handshake to goodbye.

Entering the Office and Waiting for the Interviewer

When you enter the office where the interview is to take place, introduce yourself to the receptionist. If you know the name of the person with whom you will be meeting, indicate this to the receptionist as well. If not, indicate that you have an appointment and the position you are applying for or the department is in. It is to your advantage to know the name of the person who will interview you. If possible, find out the person's name ahead of time, and be sure to write it down – it is okay to ask how to spell it. This way you can be familiar with the name to tell to the receptionist and you can use the person's name – the last name with the appropriate Mr., Mrs., Dr., etc. before it – during the interview as well.

> *While waiting in the reception area, read materials that relate to the company or job.*

Before you take a seat in the reception area to wait for your interview, try to get rid of any outdoor gear you may have with you: an outdoor-type coat, boots, or umbrella. Leave these things in the reception area if possible. Carrying them into the interview with you is awkward; it is hard to shake hands when you meet the interviewer with an umbrella in your hand. Wearing a coat into the interview makes you appear uncomfortable and as if you are ready to leave. It marks you as an outsider, since the people who belong there, the employees, are not dressed in outdoor attire.

While waiting in the reception area, review materials you brought with you if you wish, or read materials about the company if available. Reading about the company may provide information that will aid you during the interview – either help you answer questions or give you ideas for thoughtful questions you might wish to ask. If there are no company materials available, then pick up a business or news magazine while you wait. What you are seen reading also makes a statement about you, so read something worthwhile.

As the Interview Begins

When you meet the interviewer, stand up if you have been seated waiting in the reception area, smile, extend your hand, and call him or her by name if you know the person's name. Follow the interviewer from the reception area to an office, conference room, or work area where the interview will take place. Usually the interviewer will motion toward the chair where you should seat yourself. Wait for a moment for the interviewer to do this rather than just taking a seat.

Sit with a very slight forward lean toward the interviewer.

Remember the nonverbal behaviors (Chapter 6) you know are important and sit fairly erect in the chair – not like a soldier at attention, but certainly not slouching. Sit with a very slight forward lean toward the interviewer if you feel comfortable doing this. You should especially lean forward if you are particularly interested in what is being discussed or are making a point with enthusiasm. Maintain moderate eye contact with the interviewer. Try not to fidget or clench your hands together, but keep your hands relaxed and open – all the better to gesture with when you are making a point.

During the Interview

Let the interviewer begin. Listen carefully to what he says so you can learn as much as possible about the job and so you will be ready to respond to questions he may ask you. If you have prepared, you should be ready for most of the questions you are likely to be asked. If you are asked a question you were not expecting, don't panic. Ask him to repeat the question or probe for what the interviewer wants if you are unsure.

For example, if the interviewer asks you to tell him about your background, you could probe by asking whether he would like you to talk about your education or your experience. Or you could pick whichever part of your background you believe is stronger, let's say you pick your experience, talk about that briefly as it relates to the job, and then ask whether that was what he was looking for or whether he would also like to know about some other aspect – such as your education. The important thing is that you don't panic. Stay calm. Think what strength relates to the question asked and go with that. If he wants other information, he can ask a follow-up question.

Sell yourself as you answer questions posed by the interviewer.

View the interview as a two-way street. Yes, the interviewer is trying to learn about you and your potential "fit" for the job. But you need to learn as much as you can about the job – both so you can ask intelligent questions during the interview and so later, if you are offered the job, you can make your own decision about whether the job is a good "fit" for you.

Take, and perhaps even make, opportunities to sell yourself. Yes, you sell yourself as you answer questions posed by the interviewer. But if you have a real strength that relates to the job, and it doesn't seem as if the interviewer is going to ask a question that gives you the chance to sell this point, make the opportunity. Say to the interviewer, *"Let me tell you about ..."* or *"That situation reminds me of what I did at ..."* or *"When I worked at ..."* or whatever seems like a transition that gives you a chance to sell your skills, your experience, or your talent.

Listen for Underlying Messages and Questions

Of course you know you should listen to what the interviewer says and the questions you are asked. But listen at a second underlying level as well. What does the interviewer really want to know? Is the interviewer probing to try to get at the answers to questions that he is hesitant to ask or cannot ask because the questions would get into areas that are illegal to ask about?

But, you may say, if there is an area that it is illegal for the employer to ask me about, why should I volunteer information? I do not have to do that. The law is there to protect me. You are right; there are certain kinds of information you do not have to reveal. But the employer has rights too, and one of those rights is to decide not to hire you. It may often be to your advantage to choose to deal with areas of your background that you know the employer may not legally ask you about, but may know or find out about – especially if you can put a positive spin on it!

For example, an employer has the right to be interested in whether you have dependable child care so that you will be at work and on time on a regular basis. He might indirectly get to that question by asking if you anticipate any difficulties in coming to work at 8am and leaving no earlier than 5pm each day. Or he might ask if you foresee any problems in working overtime or coming in on weekends. Since you may suspect he is probing about your family situation, you might want to volunteer this information in a positive manner that also gives you information on how the employer treats employees who have a family life:

> *"I do have family obligations. But I can be flexible since I have a very supportive family. They know my work is important, and my employer usually knows how important my family is to me. I don't foresee a problem. What has been your experience in working with employees who have family obligations? Would you say this is a family-friendly company?"*

So if you have red flag areas in your background, and the employer is likely to find out about them or will at least have indications from your resume, your interview, or your references that there may be problem areas, you are usually better off to address the potential concerns in as honest, yet positive, a manner as you can.

Dealing With Questions About a Difficult Background

Prior to the interview you have anticipated areas of questioning that may involve things in your past that probably will not be plus factors in an employer's hiring decision. If you did not complete high school, are likely to receive negative comments about your work or work habits from a former employer, have a record of job hopping, have been fired from a job, have a criminal record or a record that includes alcohol or drug abuse, you must be prepared to address questions or even raise the issue yourself to put the red flag to rest and have a chance at being hired.

Chapter 10 focuses on specific questions and strategies for handling questions relating to difficult backgrounds. For now, let's look at some general guidelines for dealing with questions about red flag behaviors. You are well advised to do the following:

- Give the information asked for – no more. This is not the time to confess all your past negative behaviors. Talking too much draws excessive attention to your negatives.

- Maintain good eye contact throughout. Remember, you do not want to seem dishonest by not looking the interviewer in the eye.

- Talk briefly about what you have learned from the mistake you made in the past. Acknowledge and take responsibility for your actions.

- Talk about what you have done to change this aspect of your life. What have you done to modify the red flag situation and behavior as well as what positive behavior(s) have you put in place? Your future is different than your past.

- Make your comments positive and concise. Do not ramble on and on.

- If you are the one bringing up the subject of a red flag behavior, avoid introducing the subject early in the interview. You want to have the chance to impress the interviewer with your positive attributes and make a favorable first favorable impression. Also, avoid introducing the subject of a red flag behavior at the very end of the interview, unless you have overcome the problem in a truly significant way. You want the final thing the interviewer remembers about you to be positive.

Accentuate the Positive

You can stress your positives in part by what you say about yourself Use **positive words** such as *"I can . . . , I am interested in . . . , I have done that . . . , I was successful doing that . . . , "* Avoid negative or tentative words such as *"I can't . . . , I wouldn't . . . , or I might . . ."*

Make your statements positive and sell your strengths and your good "fit" for the job. Use specific examples when you can:

> *"At my job at ABC Co. I suggested a way to streamline stocking the shelves, and the company achieved 20% greater efficiency in this area. I was even named 'Employee of the Year'. I think my success at ABC Co. makes me a great fit for your opening in the stockroom here at XYZ Co.! I am really excited about the opportunity."*

Support your positive statements with examples – they will be remembered.

Support your positive statements with **examples and numbers**, if possible. The facts you share make your statements more credible, better understood, more interesting, and better remembered. You want to be **remembered** and want your accomplishments to be remembered after the interview is over.

Make sure your tone of voice and facial expression express the same interest and enthusiasm as your verbal message.

Ask Yourself

1. **Why are the first 4-5 minutes of the job interview so important?**

    _____

    _____

    _____

    _____

2. **What materials should you read while waiting in the reception area to meet the interviewer?**

    _____

    _____

    _____

    _____

3. **Why is it important to share examples of my past positive accomplishments with the interviewer?**

    _____

    _____

    _____

    _____

4. **Why might I want to mention a red flag behavior in my past if the employer doesn't bring it up?**

_____

_____

_____

_____

10

Handling Red Flag Questions With Savvy Answers

"Always give honest answers, but make sure the 'new you' shines through when you answer difficult questions. This is not the time to lie, shave the true, or confess your sins and ask for mercy. Tell a compelling truth – one that will get you hired!"

IF YOU HAVE ANY RED FLAGS in your background, such as those outlined in Chapter 4, be prepared to handle questions related to them. Here are some useful strategies related to sample questions and answers for dealing with such red flag issues.

No Experience

If the interviewer starts asking questions about your work experience, he might note the following:

> *"I see from your resume that you have no experience working in the landscape business. We normally hire candidates with at least one year experience. Can you tell me a little more about your experience and how it relates to this position?"*

Don't let this objection deter you from selling yourself for the position. Experience is a very relative term, and it relates to many different types of skills acquired in different settings, ranging from work to play. For example, have you worked in any volunteer positions? Did you have an internship? Don't limit your thinking to formal jobs or ones you were paid to do. If, for example, you had your own small business mowing lawns and doing yard work or if you had a paper route, you can draw on these experiences as you talk about skills you acquired, things you accomplished, and valuable experiences that prepared you for the job in question. What skills did you use in many of your life experiences?

- Interacted with clients

- Showed up when expected and on time

- Worked well with team members

- Managed time, doing hardest tasks first

- Was so successful I had to bring on a partner to help with all the business generated

Your life probably doesn't mirror this hypothetical example, but if you think hard enough, you may find you have some experiences you can use to bolster your work experience that you can talk about.

Someone following this strategy might respond to the above "lack of experience in landscaping" question by stating the following:

> *"I'm sure this is a concern since I've not previously worked for a landscape company. But let me explain where I'm coming from and why I feel I'm well suited for this position. In my previous job as well as in most tasks I undertake – be it a member of the Ravens baseball team, assistant to our church youth group, or chairman of the road maintenance committee of our community association – I'm a quick learner who understands the importance of getting things done in a well organized and timely manner. I'm a hard worker who enjoys contributing to the success of others. I believe I have the necessary experience, skills, and qualities to become a very productive member of your team. I've done lots of part-time yard work and even designed the patio and selected plants for my neighbor's back yard. I brought some pictures to show you what I did using a combination of flowering trees, scrubs, and flag stone. I love this type of work. I can assure you that my interests, attitude, enthusiasm, and drive will more than make up for my lack of formal work experience."*

Poor Grades

If an employer knows you had poor grades in school, he will most likely interpret that as a sign of failure or weakness or a lack of focus and discipline. He may or may not follow up with a question about your educational performance. Whether he asks this question or not, it will most likely be on his mind and you need to address it:

> *"C's, D's, and F's? Why didn't you do better in school?"*

Don't let this question go by without dealing with it head on. For example, did you just goof off and not take school seriously? If so, it's probably best you own up to it, accept responsibility, and indicate what an immature attitude you had at the time. If you have been in any training classes since, and you have a better record of performance, then bring that into the discussion as an indication of your maturity. On the other hand, perhaps you had extenuating circumstances, such as working 25 hours a week while going to school. Or perhaps you had a learning disorder (dyslexia, ADD, or ADHD) which was finally diagnosed, treated, and overcome. Recognizing that you had this problem and dealt with it will be a real plus in the eyes of most employers who appreciate confessions and stories about self-improvement.

An example of one good response to the "poor grades" question would be this:

"My performance in school was one of those more embarrassing periods in my life. As a kid I was very immature. I really didn't have much interest in school. I also ran around with the wrong crowd. While I could have done much better had I been more focused on learning, I did just enough to get by and have a good time with my buddies. After graduating, I spent a couple of years going from one job to another. That was a real wake-up call about my future. After two years, I decided it was time to do something else with my life. And that's when I came back to education. I wanted to go to college to study criminal justice and security, but my high school grades were too bad to get into most places. I also couldn't afford the costs, and I didn't qualify for most student loans. So I decided to take a few classes at the community college, where I could get in as well as afford the tuition. My first semester was really tough – I had to learn how to learn. But I got through with three B's – the most I had ever gotten in school! This semester I'm really enjoying my English and Computer Science classes. Although it may take me several years to finish my degree while I work full time, I'm determined to do so. Education and learning have become very important to me. I now have clearer goals and better skills which I can put to use in the security field. I just hope employers will look at what I've done since high school and my poor high school performance won't hold me back."

No Diploma

If you dropped out of high school, expect the employer to take notice and raise the obvious question:

"Why didn't you complete high school? What happened?"

After all, most people in today's workforce are expected to graduate from high school and many go on to college. People who don't graduate from high school stand out from the crowd – they are suspected of carrying some troubling baggage and may be viewed as damaged goods. High school drop-outs are generally seen as losers. They also tend to be the lowest wage earners.

If this question relates to you, make sure you're prepared with a good answer. What was your reason for dropping out of school? Did you make a mistake and are now trying to correct it? Did you have extenuating circumstances, from family to health issues? Certainly some reasons are better than others, but the bottom line is this: What are you doing or going to do about it now? Are you working on your GED? If not, why not? Having a GED or evidence that you are working on getting it suggests you are a purposeful and motivated individual.

One example of a response to this question is this:

"I'm not stupid, but I did have lots of problems in high school. I guess I was what many call a 'juvenile delinquent.' I was constantly in trouble with my parents, teachers, and local authorities. Since my attendance was so poor and I created problems for the school, I was repeatedly expelled. In fact, one teacher told me I would never amount to anything. That really made me mad – perhaps it was my wake-up call. I never

forgot what she said, and I wanted to prove her wrong. After dropping out of school, I ended up in a lot of minimum wage jobs that literally confirmed what my parents and teachers had been telling me for years – get a good education and follow your dreams. Well, being 20 years old without a high school diploma and few skills is a tough road to travel. At 20 I remembered that teacher's comment about not amounting to anything. She was right – I was headed down a very predictable road of failure. One day I literally woke up and said 'I've made a lot of mistakes, but I'm going to be somebody.' So the first thing I did was visit that teacher and ask for her help. She was great. She advised me to quickly get my GED. I immediately enrolled in a class and successfully completed my GED in June. It was a great day – I felt I had put my life back on track. Now I want to take some college courses, especially related to computer science. I love computers, and I can't wait to learn more about this fascinating field. That's why I'm so interested in this job."

Were Fired

As soon as an employer knows you have been fired, he or she is curious about why it happened:

"Why were you fired from your last job?"

"Have you been fired from other jobs?"

If you've been fired from more than one job, the employer will be concerned about a possible pattern of behavior that could be repeated in his company. No one wants to hire someone who is likely to become a problem employee requiring termination. On the other hand, being fired is not necessarily a problem. People get fired every day for all types of reasons, from routine personnel changes to serious violations of workplace rules. If the reason relates to unacceptable behavior, be sure you have a truthful and credible story indicating the problem has been dealt with and no longer exits. What was the situation? Put the best honest spin on it that you can; take responsibility for whatever negative behaviors are rightfully yours; and indicate what you have learned from the experience. Whatever you do, don't bad-mouth your former employer or put the blame on others.

A good example of a response to the firing question is this:

"I was let go at L. C. Construction Company because of my spotty attendance record. I was supposed to arrive at the work site at 6:30am. However, I often came in at 7am or 8am and sometimes as late as 1pm. Some days I didn't show up altogether, and occasionally I would disappear for two or three days without informing my supervisor. He warned me twice about my erratic behavior. Jobs weren't getting done because I couldn't be relied upon. The last time I literally disappeared for a week without contacting my supervisor. When I did finally show up, he told me my services were no longer needed and told me to clean out my locker. In fact, when I look back, I'm surprised he didn't fire me earlier. I haven't told anyone this story, because it's still

embarrassing. But here is what was really happening to me and those around me. I was going through a very difficult period in my life. I had a serious drug and alcohol abuse problem that nearly destroyed me and my family. I didn't face up to it until I got fired. The day I got fired was also the day my wife left me and moved in with her mother. She told me it was over unless I got some professional help. I had hit rock bottom and I was extremely depressed as my life fell apart. So I called my minister for counsel. He recommended that we pray together and then contact community services about a very good drug and alcohol abuse program offered through the county hospital. I just couldn't pick up the phone and make that call. I guess it meant admitting my failures and taking responsibility. He said don't worry – he would make the call and set up an appointment. What a lifesaver! This was the best thing that had happened to me in a long time. I literally surrendered to the program on the first day and religiously followed everything I was told was necessary to get rid of the demons that were controlling my life. Indeed, I got some excellent one-on-one counseling and joined a life-changing support group. I discovered I wasn't alone. I also learned how to take better control of my life by setting goals, staying focused, and following some basic time management skills. Within a couple of months I had kicked my habits and started putting my life back together. I have been doing volunteer construction work during the past two months with the Community Building Project for low income families. I haven't missed a day of work there, and I'm really making a difference in the lives of people, many who have gone through similar problems to those I encountered. Best of all, I'm back with my family and we have dreams for a new future. I also enrolled in a new home inspection program at our local community college. I should get my CRT certification by December. I can honestly say I've literally changed my life. If you hire me, you won't be inheriting my old self. While I'm now clean, I'm still part of a 12-step program, which I will continue participating in, because it has been such a great support group. It keeps me focused on taking responsibility and setting and achieving realistic goals, and it continues to remind me that this is a life-long challenge that I have to continue working at. I'm excited about the possibility of joining your company as an apprentice building inspector – always on time, dependable, and focused on results!"

Job Hopper

Employers want employees who intend to stay with them for a reasonable length of time – at least two years but ideally five years or more. While they don't expect you to

> *Employers don't want to spend time and money training you for your next employer.*

be with them a lifetime, neither do they want to spend time and money training you for your next employer. If you have a history of frequent job changes, chances are employers will view you as a potential job hopper who will most likely become a high cost liability for the company. On the other hand, some positions tend to be high turnover positions, especially in sales, restaurants, hospitality, entertainment, construction, and seasonal industries. In fact, many restaurants experience nearly a 100 percent turnover of personnel in a single year! While it's often easy to find employment in industries that have high turnover rates, it's also easy to lose a job in such industries and thus appear to be a job hopper.

The appearance of being a job hopper usually shows up on paper – on your resume or application, which includes listing your employment history. Organized chronologically, your work history indicates a pattern of behavior. If you have a history of frequent job changes, the interviewer will most likely ask you this potential knock-out question:

> *"I see from your application that you've worked for four employers during the past five years. That concerns me since our average employee has been with us for 3½ years. Why did you change jobs so often?"*

This question might be followed up with another obvious question:

> *"If we offer you this job, how long do you expect to stay with our company?"*

> *"What do you see as being different here that would cause you to stay three to five years?"*

Think carefully before you answer these questions. What were the situations? Were you fired, your company downsized, you lost interest, advanced your career, took short-term or temporary jobs for financial reasons, or worked in a high turnover industry? Whatever your situation or reasons, try to put the best face on it you honestly can and take responsibility. Here's a possible positive response to the initial question:

> *"I know four employers in five years may raise a red flag about my willingness to stay with an employer. But let me explain what happened. My first two jobs as a waiter had nothing to do with my career interests or long-term plans. They were really temporary jobs that helped me financially get through a two-year certification program in telecommunications. Upon completing the program, I landed a job with a telecommunications firm. Unfortunately, and to everyone's surprise, that company went out of business within six months. I then moved to another telecommunications firm which also went out of business within a year. I had no idea how volatile the telecommunications field was when I started school. In fact, this was one of the hottest fields around a few years ago and then the bubble burst right at the time I started my new career. I'm looking for a stable employer, such as you, who plans to be in business for a long time and who values your employees. That's what attracted me to your company. I've heard many good things about it being one of the best companies for work for in this region. I would expect to stay with you as long as possible. I see this as a place where I can grow professionally with a long and productive career working with a very exciting group of people. Given my last two jobs with companies that closed, I do have a few questions about this company and its future."*

There are many other possible scenarios relating to job hopping concerns. If you indeed are a serial job hopper who has difficulty staying with an employer for a reasonable period of time, you'll need to convince this employer that you are now different; your pattern of behavior has changed. Give examples of what you have done, as well as what you intend to do, that will make a difference. But if you look like a job hopper because you were fired from your last four jobs, you are well advised to seek professional help in dealing with what may well be some serious personal- and work-related issues.

No Focus to Jobs Held

Employers also look for candidates who seem to have a sense of purpose. They know what they want to do, set career goals, and follow through. Most employers can "read between the lines" when reviewing a candidate's work history. One thing they often look for is a pattern of career advancement. If your resume or application shows a hodge-podge of jobs held in a variety of areas and a job change did not usually result in a step up the career ladder, you have a red flag that needs careful attention. You may be asked this type of knock-out question:

> *"I noticed on your resume that you've had seven jobs during the past ten years. But they seem to be all over the place – from a cook and car salesman to repairman and security guard. Few of these jobs seem to relate to this supervisory position at our day-care center. Can you elaborate on your work history and how it relates to what we do here?"*

As you prepare for such a question, explain your situation, focus on some common elements that tie together these jobs, and note what has possibly changed in your life that has now given you renewed career direction. Here's an example of a possible response to the question:

> *"I'm glad you asked that question since it's very important that my employer understand where I'm coming from and going in the future. You're right about my background and it obviously shows. For too long I didn't know what I really wanted to do. I always seemed to be getting new work experience but little career satisfaction. After this last job, I decided it was time to do something different about my life. So I went to see a career counselor, Janet Howard, at the local One-Stop Career Center. Did I ever get an eye-opening! The first thing she asked was 'What do you want to do with the rest of your life?' I couldn't answer that question. I knew what I didn't want to do, which was what I had been doing. The next thing she did was to have me take a series of career-related tests, including the Myers-Briggs Type Indicator and Strong Interest Inventory. Based on those results, I next took a few aptitude tests and explored various career options. I then developed a detailed career plan, including what I really wanted to do over the next ten years. I now look back at my various jobs and wish I had met Ms. Howard ten years earlier! However, I also learned that I did gain some valuable experience in those jobs that do directly relate to my career plans. In particular, I often supervised people and really enjoyed this aspect of these jobs. Since I also love kids, I couldn't think of a better job to launch my new career. By the way, I didn't put Ms. Howard down as one of my references, but you may want to talk to her about my testing results. She knows a great deal about my skills, interests, and aptitudes that would be relevant to this job."*

Poor References

Expect to be asked for references and expect employers to contact your previous employers for information about you. If you have some skeletons in the closet with previous employers, it's time you take some important actions to ensure that they do not become killer references.

Since references are normally checked between the period you are interviewed and offered the job, you may never have a chance to address any red flag questions arising from what your references say about you. Therefore, it's extremely important that you choose your references well so that no unexpected red flags get tossed your way during this critical decision-making phase. Think hard and try to identify some people who will give you a good reference (other than your relatives!). By carefully selecting, you may be able to salvage this one.

Try to select references that fall into the following categories:

- **Former employers:** Can verify your work history and talk about your accomplishments and pattern of work behavior. If you have former employers who may speak ill of you, heed the advice at the end of this section.

- **Character witness:** An associate, minister, or someone else who you have worked with who can speak about your good character.

If you have a difficult background and you know the employer knows this, include a reference who can testify to how you have turned your life around. If, for example, you were recently incarcerated and appear rehabilitated, this person might be a prison minister, chief psychologist, education officer, or parole officer – not a former inmate.

When you go to the job interview, make sure you have a list of references to give to the interviewer. If they don't appear on your application, the interviewer will most likely ask for your references during the interview. Consequently, it's always a good idea to contact your references *before* sharing them with an employer. Let your potential references know you are conducting a job search and ask for their permission to serve as a reference. Give them a copy of your resume, or a summary of your background, and tell them they may be called by a few employers who will be checking you out. Go one step further and ask if they could serve as a **favorable** reference. The more information you give them about yourself and how you fit the position in question, the better prepared they will be to give you a good reference.

Let's talk about one type of reference you might want to avoid, because he or she could be potentially damaging to your future – a former employer who fired you or one you left in a huff. In fact, the interviewer may ask you if it's okay for her to contact your former employer. If you say *"no,"* you raise a red flag. Be ready to say *"yes"* to such requests. This may be the time to mend some old broken fences. If you left a position under difficult circumstances, it may be to your benefit to make up with your former employer. Turn any anger into forgiveness. Call him and make amends for any ill feelings. Time has passed, both you and he have changed, and it's time to get on with your life. Chances are he will be receptive to this gesture. Tell him what you have been doing since you left, what changes have taken place, and ask if he will be willing to serve as a favorable reference. Regardless of the circumstances of your leaving this employer, in the end most employers wish their former employees the best, even though they might never hire them again. They understand the culture of references – stress the positives and overlook the negatives. After all, we all need to get on with our lives, and fresh starts are great ways to unload heavy baggage that may continue to drag you down. Approached in this manner, that former employer may become one of your strongest supporters and advocates in the reference department!

Ex-Offender

As we noted at the beginning of this book, statistics tell an important, sobering, and often whispered story. People with criminal backgrounds have some of the brightest red flags flying. In the United States over 2 million people are currently incarcerated; 650,000 people are annually released on probation; over 5 million people remain on parole or probation; and over 77 million people have some type of conviction on their record. While not widely publicized, a large percentage of local government employment programs (Workforce Development) are aimed at helping ex-offenders transition to the world of work. Baltimore, Maryland, for example, alone absorbs over 80,000 ex-offenders each year. Ex-offenders present special challenges for career counselors, who must deal with many types of red flag behaviors, ranging from murder to assault. And many ex-offenders become known as local sex offenders with limited employment opportunities.

> *Employers want to hire rehabilitated ex-offenders who take responsibility and do not pose problems for the employer and fellow employees*

That's millions of red flags waving in front of employers! So why would an employer want to hire someone with a criminal background? The answer is simple: Thousands of employers hire ex-offenders each day, because they have desirable skills and work habits; many also work for very low wages and are very loyal. But they want to hire *rehabilitated ex-offenders* who take responsibility and do not pose problems for the employer and fellow employees.

The first knock-out question most ex-offenders face often appears on an application form or in the job interview:

"Have you ever been convicted of a felony? If yes, give details."

If you have been convicted, how should you best respond to this question on an application form? You basically have four choices:

1. Lie by saying *"no."*

2. Don't respond – just leave it blank and go on to another question.

3. Be truthful by saying *"yes"* and give the details.

4. Be truthful by saying *"yes"* and then follow up by saying *"details provided at the interview."*

Whatever you do, don't lie. Lying will just delay the inevitable – the employer will most likely find out about your conviction during a background check. Leaving the question unanswered implies you may have something to hide, although your non-response to this question may be overlooked and the question may never again be raised. Writing about the details gives you little opportunity to explain what happened and what changes have taken place since your conviction. Your best course of action would be to inform the employer that you will provide details at the interview. You want to do this because you need to be in control of the story relating to your conviction.

The good news is that you may never see this discriminatory question appear on an application form. More and more states, counties, and cities "ban the box" on applications because it is a form of minority discrimination. But you're not out of the woods. Instead, the "conviction" question is likely to arise during a face-to-face interview.

Once you get to the interview, the interviewer may ask you details about your conviction. This is the time to do two things:

1. **Take responsibility for your actions.** Whatever you do, don't retry your case, blame your problems on others, and talk on and on about the problem. Your listener is not really interested in learning all the details, which may be scary to some people who are not used to dealing with ex-offenders. Give a very brief overview of what happened to you – the crime, the conviction, the outcome. You should be able to do this within one minute. Remember, DON'T TALK TOO MUCH! Share the basic facts and move on to higher ground.

2. **Focus on how you have changed your life for the better because of this experience.** Remember, the employer wants to **hire your future** – not your past. Let him know that you are a mature, trustworthy, and loyal individual who has the requisite motivation, attitudes, and skills to do the job in question. You've learned important life lessons. Now you want to get on with a new and productive life. You only ask that the employer give you a chance to earn his trust and prove your value. This part of your story may take three to five minutes. But again, don't talk too much – just enough to let the employer know you are a new and potentially very productive person.

Employers are like many other people – sympathetic to individuals who have made mistakes but who are willing to take responsibility and make sincere efforts to change

> *We live in a culture of forgiveness, redemption, and self-transformation.*

their lives. It's part of our culture of forgiveness, redemption, and self- transformation. After all, we all make mistakes, although some are more egregious errors than others. We all want to believe in the power of self-transformation – the ability to break out of self-destructive patterns of behavior and create a new life based upon new attitudes, motivations, and goals. Whatever you do, make sure you stress your future rather than dwell on your past. Again, employers want to hire your future, despite your past.

Here's an instructive example of an ex-offender's response to the conviction question:

> *"Yes, I had problems when I was 18. I was convicted of car theft and drug possession. At the time I was a high school dropout, unemployed, and ran around with the wrong crowd. Needless to say, I was very immature and stupid. I pled guilty and was given a 10-year sentence at Morain Correctional Institution. Within a few weeks I knew I had hit rock bottom. I was surprised how many fellow inmates were repeat offenders – their whole life was one big and bad revolving door of talking big, getting into more trouble, and doing more time. The stuff that went on there was scary. I didn't want to be a part of that group. By chance I had an opportunity to work in the library. For the first time in my life I was surrounded by a forest of books. While I did not finish school, I was a good reader. Those books soon became my best new friends. In the library one day I picked up a book entitled **Living Life on Purpose and With Meaning**. Wow! It literally changed my life. Indeed, I was determined to change my life and never again come in contact with the criminal justice system. I wanted to be out for good and to dream dreams I never had. The first thing I did was to share my thoughts with the librarian who had taken special interest in me. She suggested I get my GED and then she recommended a good reading list to help me better plan my life, from inspirational books to materials on alternative careers for people without a four-year degree. Within a year I got my GED and then enrolled in the prison college program where I soon discovered I had a good aptitude for electrical engineering. I couldn't believe how much I loved learning. This opened a whole new world to me. With the help of my teachers, the chief psychologist, and the librarian – and my parents who stood by me doing this difficult period in my life – I was able to turn what appeared to be a very bad situation, incarceration, into one of the best things that ever happened to me. Within three years I was released on good behavior. I've definitely matured. I have a wonderful girl friend who is a teacher, and I'm continuing to take courses at the community college. I hope to complete my Associate Degree in Electrical Engineering within the next three years. I'm very excited about eventually becoming an electrical engineering technician with your company. Right now I'm looking at my future, but I'm also well aware that I have some baggage that will be with me the rest of my life. I'm just hoping that employers will look at what I've done with my life during the past three years rather than when I was 18 and give me a chance to prove that I will become one of their most valuable employees."*

But let's also acknowledge that some criminal activities are difficult to deal with in the job market. For example, if you have been convicted of assault, murder, or a sex crime, your red flag is bigger than most red flags of ex-offenders. These are frightening crimes for many employers who do not want the liability of such individuals working next to other employees. If you've done time for such crimes, you'll need to put together a **rehabilitation portfolio** as well as seek jobs with employers who are known to work with such ex-offenders.

On the other hand, if you've not made important behavioral changes, it's time to take responsibility and reach out for assistance. If you fail to do that, expect more bad things to happen to you in the future, especially when it comes to finding and keeping a job and maintaining good relationships.

Abused Drugs or Alcohol

No one wants to hire someone with a drug or alcohol abuse problem. After all, these problems plague many companies, which already spend millions of dollars each year on employee assistance programs designed to rehabilitate workers who abuse substances, and hence themselves. Many companies now require drug testing as a condition of employment. If you've ever walked into a Home Depot, you'll even see a sign posted at the entry for would-be applicants: *"We require drug tests of all candidates."* If you have a drug or alcohol problem, chances are you also have other problems that are best treated with professional help.

Most employers will not ask you about your drug and alcohol practices. Instead, they will see if you are drug free when they send you off for a drug test. However, drug and alcohol abuse problems tend to manifest themselves in other behavior problems related to the workplace – erratic work habits, low performance, excessive sick days, lack of focus, frequent job changes, and being fired. A good example of how to deal with this issue was covered in the earlier example under "Were Fired." Again, your best strategy is to come clean by taking responsibility and explaining what you have done to change your life so that substance abuse is no longer a problem for you and an employer in the workplace. Forgiveness, redemption, and self-transformation apply equally to this red flag issue as it does to many issues related to ex-offenders.

Over-Qualified

Many employers receive resumes and applications from individuals who appear over-qualified for the position being filled. Some are tempted to interview such individuals simply because they have much to offer given the level of the position. But such employers also must be realistic. Someone who appears over-qualified for the position will most likely be a problem employee. The person may not be happy working beneath his or her skill and pay level. As a result, the person may quickly leave when a better opportunity comes along. Such people may also be hiding an employment problem, such as being fired. On a more positive note, the individual may be in the process of changing careers and thus what initially appears as over-qualifications may be nothing more than an attempt to start a new career involving a new set of interests and skills. Indeed, it's not unusual for individuals to change careers two to three times during their worklife.

Whatever the case, the employer may raise this potential red flag question:

> *"You have an impressive resume. But one thing really concerns me. You appear over-qualified for this position. Why are you particularly interested in an entry-level production job when you have such an extensive managerial background?"*

In reading between the lines, the interviewer is really raising an objection to hiring you: You won't be happy here and you won't stay long. Knowing this, your strategy should be to alleviate any doubts in the interviewer's mind that you really want this job. Be truthful, transparent, and enthusiastic. An example of an excellent response to this question is this:

> *"You're right. I do appear over-qualified for this position. In fact, I had a real problem writing a resume that indicated what I really wanted to do next in my life. My resume shouts 'Manager.' Given my more than 20 years of progressive management experience, it would appear I would be looking for a $125,000+ a year senior management position. But that's not what I really want to do in the future. Over the years I enjoyed the work and accomplished a lot in various management positions. During the last six months I began reassessing what I really wanted to do with the rest of my life. The answer was not to become another manager. I've been there, done that. Now I want to do something more personally and professionally rewarding. And money is no longer a major concern – the kids have graduated from college and we recently paid off the house mortgage. I now feel comfortable changing careers. I want to do something more creative and in line with my artistic interests. In fact, for many years I've had a wonderful and fascinating hobby – photography. I've taken numerous photos and even won an award in a travel magazine last year for a monastery shot I took on a photo tour to Bhutan last year. I brought my portfolio with me to show you samples of my work. I simply want to become a well respected professional photographer. I don't want to manage anyone or anything – just take great photos and contribute to the success of your studio. I also would be happy to share any of my management experience with you should it be relevant to this company. Could I show you my portfolio? I'm sure it won't make me look over-qualified, but I think it will tell you my story better than my resume."*

Questions You Should Ask

One of the most important questions you can answer is that last one on our list of 101 questions – *"Do you have any questions?"* The answer should be *"Yes, I have a few questions."* No matter how thorough the interview, no matter how much give-and-take, you should have at least two or three questions to ask near the end of the interview. In fact, not asking any questions may hurt your chances of getting the job offer. During the interview other questions will probably come to mind which you had not anticipated.

When asked whether you have questions, you may indicate that many have been answered thus far, but you have a few additional questions. You should have jotted some questions down as you prepared for your interview. Feel free to refer to that list if you need to at this point. The fact that you have given thought to this aspect of the interview and have come prepared will be viewed as a positive by the interviewer. You may have questions, for example, about the relationship of this job to other significant functional areas in the company; staff development; training programs; career advancement opportunities; the extent to which promotions are from within the organization; how employee performance is evaluated; or the expected growth of the company. You may want to ask questions that probe areas that were touched on earlier during the interview. For example, if the interviewer has mentioned that the company has an excellent training program, you may have specific questions: What kinds of training would you be offered? How frequently? How long do most training programs last?

> *You should have at least two or three questions to ask near the end of the interview.*

If you are still interested in this job, be sure to close the interview by summarizing the strong points you would bring to the position and indicate your continued interest in the job and the company. Ask what the next step will be and when they expect to make a decision. Follow the advice in the next chapter on closing and following up the interview. If you follow this process from beginning to end with intelligent answers and questions, you'll go a long way to getting the job offer despite your not-so-hot background!

Ask Yourself

1. **Which job interview questions do I feel most uncomfortable answering?**

_____

_____

_____

_____

2. **Why would someone want to hire me?**

_____

_____

_____

_____

3. **How can I best answer this initial question:** *"Tell me about yourself."*

_____

_____

_____

_____

4. **What are my three greatest strengths that I would bring to the workplace?**

_____

_____

_____

_____

5. **Which red flag questions might I be asked based upon reviewing my resume and/or application?**

_____

_____

_____

_____

6. **What is the best way to answer each of those potential knock-out questions?**

_____

_____

_____

_____

7. **What questions should I ask the interviewer?**

_____

_____

_____

_____

11

Closing and Following Up the Interview

"Two of the best kept secrets to getting a job offer is the quality of your closing and your choice of follow-up activities. Neglect closing and follow up and you can kiss your interview goodbye!"

WHAT DO YOU PLAN TO DO when the interview is over? Say thank you, get up, leave, and then wait to hear if you're the chosen one? When is the job interview really over? Beyond answering and asking questions, what other actions can you take to influence the outcome of the interview?

This chapter reveals a variety of tips that relate to two of the most important, yet neglected, phases of the job interview – close and follow up. If you want to get invited back to another interview and offered the job, you must engage in certain self-serving activities. Indeed, you must take initiative in asking for the job.

Summarize and Restate Your Interest

Interviewers normally will initiate the close by standing, shaking hands, and thanking you for coming to the interview. They may express some variation of *"Glad you could come by today. We have several other candidates to interview. We'll be in touch."* In response, most interviewees shake hands, thank the interviewer, leave, and hope for the best. Don't do this!

Hope is not a good job search strategy. And neither is **waiting**.

At this stage, you should **summarize** the interview in terms of your interests, strengths, and goals. Briefly restate your qualifications and continuing interest in working with the employer. For example, an accountant might summarize the interview as follows:

> *I'm really glad I had the chance to talk with you. I know, with what I learned when I reorganized the accounting department at XYZ Corporation, I could increase your profits, too.*

Don't Play Competitive Games

Anxious to receive a job offer at the end of the interview, some candidates feel compelled to interject an element of competition into the closing of the interview by indicating they either have, or expect to soon receive an offer from another company. If this is true and you are under pressure to make a decision, let this employer know about your time-sensitive situation. You might say the following:

> *I want to let you know that I've received a job offer from another company that is expecting me to make a decision within the next two days. Is there any chance you could let know your decision by Thursday? I really prefer this job, but I need to soon respond to the offer.*

If you are only interviewing with other companies and have not received a job offer, avoid playing the hard-to-get game. It would be dishonest for you to indicate you have a job offer when in fact you do not. Trying to put pressure on the employer to quickly offer you the job could backfire – the employer may decide to "let you go."

Ask for the Job If You Really Want It

One of the most effective closings is to simply ask for the job. In fact, employers want to hire candidates who are **enthusiastic** about their company and who want to work with them. You can ask for the job in several different ways. The following examples are designed to help you formulate a close that best fits your situation:

> *Even though I'm looking at other opportunities, this is really the place I would love to work. It's where I know I can make a difference.*

> *I'll be very disappointed if you don't hire me! This is the place where I really want to build both a company and a career.*

> *I've always dreamt of working in such an innovative company where employees are considered family. If you offer me the job, I can guarantee within six months you'll see a big change in your bottom line.*

Ask for Permission to Follow Up

Ask the interviewer when he or she expects to make the hiring decision. If the response is *"Friday of next week,"* then ask, *"If I haven't heard by the following Monday, may I give you a call?"* Almost everyone will say you may, and you will have solved your problem of wondering when you will hear about the final decision and what to do next.

If you haven't heard anything by the time the designated Monday arrives, do call. Some interviewers use this technique to see if you will follow through with a call – others are just inconsiderate.

By taking the initiative in this manner, the employer will be prompted to clarify your status soon, and you will have an opportunity to talk again.

Prepare a List of References

Many interviewers will ask you for a list of references. Be sure to prepare such a list **prior to** the interview. Include the names, addresses, and phone numbers of four individuals who will give you positive professional and personal recommendations. If asked for references, you will appear well prepared by presenting a list in this manner. If you fail to prepare this information ahead of time, you may appear at best disorganized and at worst lacking good references. Always anticipate being asked for specific names, addresses, and phone numbers of your references.

References are not the same as **letters of recommendation**. Some people may advise you to put together a portfolio of letters from individuals who praise your skills, qualifications, and work behavior. They suggest presenting their testimonials during the interview. I'm not a big fan of such self-serving activities, which could backfire on candidates. After all, it's borderline manipulation. Employers aren't stupid. They know such glowing letters presented by you have been carefully selected to put your best foot forward. If an employer wants recommendations, he'll contact individuals on your list to get more candid information about your patterns of workplace behavior and character.

Make Follow-Up a Top Priority

Follow-up is a much neglected art, but it is the key to unlocking employers' doors and for achieving job search success. But many people fear following up. Like giving a speech, it requires initiating communications with strangers! Unfortunately, many interviewees would rather wait to hear from the employer than to take actions that could influence the final hiring decision. Here's a simple truth – waiting is not a good job search strategy!

Follow-up occurs at the implementation stage of your job search. Without an effective follow-up campaign, you may be passed over for the job. If you want interviewers to know that you are interested in their position, you need to follow up with a nice thank-you letter and/or phone call, in which you restate your strongest talents. At this stage, timing is everything.

Send a Thank-You Letter

Shortly after the interview – later the same day or the next day at the latest – send a thank-you letter by e-mail and mail. In this letter:

1. Express your appreciation for the time the interviewer(s) spent with you
2. Indicate your continued interest in the position.
3. Restate any special skills or experience you would bring to the job (keep this brief and well focused).
4. Close by mentioning that you will call in a few days to inquire about the employer's decision.

Send the e-mail within 24-hours of completing the interview. Follow it with a mailed copy of the e-mail in formal letter form, which you need to send by snail-mail. Remember, this is a business letter and the stationery, format, and writing style should reflect your professionalism. The letter should be typed – not handwritten – on good quality bond paper. Page 103 includes an example of such a thank-you letter. For additional examples of letters, see my companion volumes, *Nail the Cover Letter!* and *201 Dynamite Job Search Letters*.

Follow Through With a Telephone Call

Remember (page 101) at the end of the interview you asked when a decision would be made, and asked whether you could call if you hadn't heard within a couple of days of that date? Don't just ask the question and leave it at that – you must follow through. If the decision date has passed, make the follow-up call.

If no decision has yet been made, your call will remind them of your continued interest. You also should impress the employer as someone who does follow through, and he could expect this same commitment from you as an employee. If the employer has made a decision and was about to call and offer you the position, that's great! If someone else has been offered the job you may be disappointed, but it is just as well to find out now and concentrate your job search efforts elsewhere than to waste time waiting to hear about this job.

Ask Yourself

1. **You're near the end of a 30-minute job interview. The interviewer decides it's time to conclude the interview by saying *"Well, I think that covers everything. I want to thank you for coming in today."* What do you say in response to this signal that the job interview is now ending?**

_____

_____

_____

_____

_____

_____

_____

_____

_____

_____

_____

_____

Thank-You Letter
Post-Job Interview

2962 Forrest Drive
Denver, Colorado 82171
May 28, 20

Terry Wilson
Director, Personnel Department
Denver Landscape Artists
7229 Lakewood Drive
Denver, Colorado 82170

Dear Mr. Wilson:

Thank you again for the opportunity to interview for the landscape design position. I appreciated your hospitality and enjoyed meeting you and members of your staff.

The interview convinced me of how compatible my background, interest, and skills are with the goals of Denver Landscape Artists. My prior landscape experience as well as recent landscape design training has prepared me to take a major role in developing nontraditional stone patios and fountains. I am confident we would work well together in producing excellent design work and attracting new clientele to your company.

As you suggested, I'll give you a call Thursday afternoon to see if you've made a decision. In the meantime, if you have any additional questions, please let me know. I look forward to meeting you again, hopefully as a member of your team.

Sincerely,

Tim Potter

Tim Potter
pottert@mymail.com

2. **It has been a week and you still haven't heard from the employer. This is a job you really want. What should you do at this point other than wait some more?**

_____

_____

_____

_____

_____

_____

_____

_____

_____

_____

_____

_____

3. **You call the employer and learn that a hiring decision has not yet been made. So what do you say and do?**

_____

_____

_____

_____

_____

_____

_____

_____

_____

_____

_____

_____

12

Deal Effectively With Job Offers and Compensation

"Never talk about money and benefits until you've been offered the job. Always remember this simple principle: He who talks about money first tends to lose the advantage. If you want to make more money, keep your mouth shut and negotiate smart!"

IN THE END, IT'S ALL ABOUT MONEY and related benefits. The job interview process is not over until you get a job offer and then agree on fair compensation for your talent. However, many job seekers make several salary mistakes, from not knowing their worth and prematurely discussing salary to failing to properly negotiate a compensation package that truly reflects their value in today's job market. Part of the problem is **cultural** – reluctance to talk about money and other people's salaries. But the major problem relates to the lack of compensation information and weak salary negotiation skills.

Ex-Offenders and Compensation

The tips in this chapter introduce you to the major issues relating to salary and job offers. While many ex-offenders re-entering the free world may have little negotiation leverage when seeking their first job out, which is not unusual for anyone in a transitional situation (such as students, military, Peace Corps, homemakers, retirees re-entering the workforce in new careers), nonetheless, they should be aware of important compensation options that will have an impact on them and their families in the future.

When you accept a job, you basically agree to a certain cash flow amount to manage your finances and invest in your future. Accepting a job offer is serious business that can make or break you financially. While many ex-offenders will take any job offered, especially non-negotiable minimum wage positions because they fear being unemployed and financially destitute, nonetheless, the skills outlined in this chapter hopefully will come in very handy at some point in your future employment history. Indeed, they should be worth thousands of dollars in income over the coming years.

105

For more information on how to become a savvy salary negotiator, see my three companion volumes: *Give Me More Money*, *Salary Negotiation Tips for Professionals*, and *Get a Raise in 7 Days*.

Most Salaries Are Negotiable

Contrary to what many job seekers believe, salary is seldom predetermined except for entry-level and minimum wage positions. Most employers have some flexibility to negotiate salary and benefits. While few employers try to blatantly exploit applicants (some do, especially in minimum wage positions), neither do they want to pay applicants more than what they have to or what a candidate will accept.

Salaries are usually assigned to positions or jobs rather than to individuals. But not everyone is of equal value in performing the job; some are more productive than others. Since individual performance differs, you should attempt to establish your **value** in the eyes of the employer rather than accept a salary figure for the job. The art of salary negotiation will help you do this.

Become a Savvy Salary Negotiator

Just how savvy a salary negotiator are you? How prepared are you to negotiate a salary that truly reflects your worth? What knowledge and skills do you need to become a savvy salary negotiator?

Let's start by evaluating your knowledge and skill level for becoming an effective salary negotiator. Respond to the following statements by circling "Yes" or "No." If you are uncertain about your answer, just leave the statement alone and move on to the next statement. While some of these questions relate to individuals who are currently employed or are in white-collar professional positions, try to respond to these statements as well as you can.

Your Salary Negotiation I.Q.

1. I know what I'm worth in comparison to others in today's
    job market.   Yes   No

2. I know what others make in my company.   Yes   No

3. I can negotiate a salary 15 percent higher than my current salary.   Yes   No

4. I can negotiate a salary 5-10 percent higher than what the
    employer is prepared to offer me.   Yes   No

5. I know where I can quicky find salary information for my
    particular industry and position.   Yes   No

6. I usually feel comfortable talking about compensation issues
    with others, including my boss.   Yes   No

7. I understand the different types of stock options and equity incentives offered by employers in my field. Yes No

8. I'm familiar with how various compensation options work with most employers, such as signing bonuses, performance bonuses, cafeteria plans, reimbursement accounts, disability insurance, 401(k) plans, SEPs, CODAs, stock options, flex-time, tuition reimbursements, and severance pay. Yes No

9. I know what my current compensation package is worth when translated into dollar equivalents. Yes No

10. I'm prepared to negotiate more than seven different compensation options. Yes No

11. I have a list of at least 50 accomplishments and a clear patternof performance which I can communicate to prospective employers. Yes No

12. I'm prepared to tell at least five different one- to three-minute stories about my proudest professional achievements. Yes No

13. If asked to state my "salary requirements" in a cover letteror on an application, I know what to write. Yes No

14. I know when I should and should not discuss salary during an interview. Yes No

15. I know what to say if the interviewer asks me, *"What are your salary expectations?"* Yes No

16. I know what questions to ask during the interview in order to get information about salaries in the interviewer's company. Yes No

17. I know when it's time to stop talking and start serious negotiations. Yes No

18. I know how to use the "salary range" to create "common ground" and strengthen my negotiation position. Yes No

19. I know how to use silence to strengthen my negotiation position. Yes No

20. If offered a position, I know what to say and do next. Yes No

TOTALS _____ _____

If you responded "No" to more than three of the above statements or "Yes" to fewer than 15 of the statements, you need to work on developing your salary negotiation skills.

Avoid 21 Salary Negotiation Mistakes

Job seekers typically make several salary negotiation errors, which often result in knocking them out of consideration for the job or they receive and accept a lower salary than what they could have gotten had they practiced a few of the salary tips outlined in this chapter. Several of these errors also may leave a bad impression with an employer – that you have a poor attitude, or you are basically a self-centered job seeker who primarily focuses on salary and benefits rather than on the performance needs of the employer and organization. The most frequent errors you should avoid include:

1. Engage in wishful thinking – believing you are worth a lot more than you are currently being paid but having no credible evidence to support this belief.

2. Approach the job search as an exercise in being clever and manipulative rather than being clear, correct, and competent in communicating your value to others.

3. Fail to research salary options and comparables and thus having few supports to justify your worth.

4. Fail to compile a list of accomplishments, including anecdotal one- to three-minute performance stories, that provide evidence of your value to employers.

5. Reveal salary expectations on the resume or in a letter.

6. Answer the question *"What are your salary requirements?"* before being offered the job.

7. Raise the salary question rather than waiting for the employer to do so.

8. Fail to ask questions about the company, job, and previous occupants of the position.

9. Ask *"Is this offer negotiable?"*

10. Quickly accept the first offer, believing that's what the position is really worth and that an employer might be offended if you try to negotiate.

11. Accept the offer on the spot.

12. Accept the offer primarily because of compensation.

13. Try to negotiate compensation during the first interview.

14. Forget to calculate the value of benefits and thus only focus on the gross salary figure.

15. Focus on benefits, stock options, and perks rather than on the gross salary figure.

16. Negotiate a salary figure rather discuss a salary range.

17. Negotiate over the telephone or by e-mail.

18. Talk too much and listen too little.

19.   Focus on your needs rather than the employer's needs.

20.   Try to play "hardball."

21.   Express a negative attitude toward the employer's offer.

Don't Discuss Salary Before Receiving an Offer

Employers often raise the salary question early in the interview. They may actually do this during a telephone screening interview. Their basic goal is to either screen you into or out of consideration for the position on salary criteria. Like stating your salary expectations on a resume or in a cover letter, responding to this question with a figure early in the interview puts you at a disadvantage. The old poker saying that *"He who reveals his hand first is at a disadvantage"* is especially true when negotiating salary.

Time should work in your favor. After all, you need more information about the job and your responsibilities in order to determine the value of the position. What is the job really worth? A job worth $75,000 a year has different levels of responsibility than one worth only $30,000 a year. If the employer raises the salary expectation questions early in the interview, it's best to respond by saying *"I really need to know more about the position and my responsibilities before I can discuss compensation. Can you tell me about . . . ?"* This response will usually result in postponing the salary question and impress upon the employer that you are a thoughtful person who is more employer-centered than self-centered with your interest in the position.

> *Salary should be the very last thing you talk about – after you receive a job offer.*

Salary should be the very last thing you talk about – within the context of a job offer, which may not occur during the first interview. Once you have been offered the job, then it's time to talk about compensation.

Let the Employer Volunteer Salary Information

Today, many candidates go through three to seven interviews with an employer before receiving a job offer. Except for some entry-level positions, the first interview seldom deals with the money question, although this question can arise at any time to screen someone into or out of consideration. You should never raise the salary issue, for to do so puts you at a disadvantage. Expect the salary offer, and accompanying salary negotiations, to take place during the final interview.

The signal that you should talk seriously about money is when you are offered the job. The offer comes first followed by discussion of appropriate compensation. Another way of handling the *"What are your salary requirements?"* question is to respond by asking, *"Are you offering me the position?"* If the response is *"No,"* then you might respond by saying, *"I really need to know more about the position and your company before I feel comfortable discussing compensation."* Alternatively, you might want to use this occasion to do research on the company's salary structure by asking, *"By the way, how much are you paying at present for this position?"* Always try to get the employer to volunteer salary information from which you can formulate your response.

Examine the Total Compensation Package

One of the easiest ways to survey your options and assign value to your ideal compensation package is to use the following checklist of options. Consider those items that related to your employment situation (maybe only 20 percent are relevant) and then value it by assigning a dollar amount. When finished, add up the total dollars assigned to get a complete picture of the value of your present or past compensation package.

Element	Value
Basic Compensation Issues	
❏ Base salary	$ _____
❏ Commissions	$ _____
❏ Corporate profit sharing	$ _____
❏ Personal performance bonuses/incentives	$ _____
❏ Cost of living adjustment	$ _____
❏ Overtime	$ _____
❏ Signing bonus	$ _____
❏ Cash in lieu of certain benefits	$ _____
Health Benefits	
❏ Medical insurance	$ _____
❏ Dental insurance	$ _____
❏ Vision insurance	$ _____
❏ Prescription package	$ _____
❏ Life insurance	$ _____
❏ Accidental death and disability insurance	$ _____
❏ Evacuation insurance (international travel)	$ _____
Vacation and Time Issues	
❏ Vacation time	$ _____
❏ Sick days	$ _____
❏ Personal time	$ _____
❏ Holidays	$ _____
❏ Flex-time	$ _____
❏ Compensatory time	$ _____

❑   Paternity/maternity leave $ _____
❑   Family leave $ _____

Retirement-Oriented Benefits

❑   Defined benefit plan $ _____
❑   401(k) plan $ _____
❑   Deferred compensation $ _____
❑   Savings plans $ _____
❑   Stock-purchase plans $ _____
❑   Stock bonus $ _____
❑   Stock options $ _____
❑   Ownership/equity $ _____

Education

❑   Professional continuing education $ _____
❑   Tuition reimbursement for you or your family members $ _____

Military

❑   Compensatory pay during active duty $ _____
❑   National Guard $ _____

Perquisites

❑   Cellular phone $ _____
❑   Company car or vehicle/mileage allowance $ _____
❑   Expense accounts $ _____
❑   Liberalization of business-related expenses $ _____
❑   Child care $ _____
❑   Cafeteria privileges $ _____
❑   Executive dining room privileges $ _____
❑   First-class hotels $ _____
❑   First-class air travel $ _____
❑   Upgrade business travel $ _____
❑   Personal use of frequent-flyer awards $ _____
❑   Convention participation: professionally related $ _____
❑   Parking $ _____
❑   Paid travel for spouse $ _____
❑   Professional association memberships $ _____
❑   Athletic club memberships $ _____
❑   Social club memberships $ _____

❏   Use of company-owned facilities $ _____
❏   Executive office $ _____
❏   Office with a window $ _____
❏   Laptop computers $ _____
❏   Private secretary $ _____
❏   Employee discounts $ _____
❏   Incentive trips $ _____
❏   Sabbaticals $ _____
❏   Discounted buying club memberships $ _____
❏   Free drinks and meals $ _____

Relocation Expenses

❏   Direct moving expenses $ _____
❏   Moving costs for unusual property $ _____
❏   Trips to find suitable housing $ _____
❏   Loss on sale of present home or lease termination $ _____
❏   Company handling sale of present home $ _____
❏   Housing cost differential between cities $ _____
❏   Mortgage rate differential $ _____
❏   Mortgage fees and closing costs $ _____
❏   Temporary dual housing $ _____
❏   Trips home during dual residency $ _____
❏   Real estate fees $ _____
❏   Utilities hookup $ _____
❏   Drapes/carpets $ _____
❏   Appliance installation $ _____
❏   Auto/pet shipping $ _____
❏   Signing bonus for incidental expenses $ _____
❏   Additional meals expense account $ _____
❏   Bridge loan while owning two homes $ _____
❏   Outplacement assistance for spouse $ _____

Home Office Options

❏   Personal computer $ _____
❏   Internet access $ _____
❏   Copier $ _____
❏   Printer $ _____
❏   Financial planning assistance $ _____

- ❏ Separate phone line $ _____
- ❏ Separate fax line $ _____
- ❏ CPA/tax assistance $ _____
- ❏ Incidental/support office functions $ _____
- ❏ Office supplies $ _____
- ❏ Furniture and accessories $ _____

Severance Packages (Parachutes)

- ❏ Base salary $ _____
- ❏ Bonuses/incentives $ _____
- ❏ Non-compete clause $ _____
- ❏ Stock/equity $ _____
- ❏ Outplacement assistance $ _____
- ❏ Voice mail access $ _____
- ❏ Statement (letter) explaining why you left $ _____
- ❏ Vacation reimbursement $ _____
- ❏ Health benefits or reimbursements $ _____
- ❏ 401(k) contributions $ _____

                                                  TOTAL $ _____

Focus on Salary Ranges

Savvy salary negotiators always talk about "salary ranges" rather than specific salary figures. They do so because ranges give them flexibility to negotiate. If, for example, the employer reveals his hand first by saying the job pays $35,000 a year, you could counter by putting the employer's figure at the bottom of your range – *"Based on my salary research as well as my experience, I was expecting between $40,000 and $45,000 a year."* By doing this, you **establish common ground** from which to negotiate the figure upwards toward the high end of your range.

> *Establish common ground from which to negotiate the figure upwards toward the high end of the range.*

While the employer may not want to pay more than $40,000, he or she at least knows you are within budget. The employer most likely will counter by saying, *"Well, we might be able to go $42,000."* You, in turn, can counter by saying *"Is it possible to go to $44,000?"* As you will quickly discover in the salary negotiation business, anything is "possible" if you handle the situation professionally – with supports and flexibility. In this situation, you might be able to negotiate a $4,000 increase over the employer's initial offer because you establish common ground with a salary range and then move the employer toward the upper end of your range because you had supports and professional appeal.

Carefully Examine Benefits

Many employers will try to impress candidates with the benefits offered by the company. These might include retirement, bonuses, stock options, medical and life insurance, and cost of living adjustments. If the employer includes these benefits in the salary negotiations, do not be overly impressed. Most benefits are standard – they come with the job. When negotiating salary, it is best to talk about specific dollar figures. But don't neglect to both calculate and negotiate benefits according to the checklist on pages 98-100.

Benefits can translate into a significant portion of one's compensation, especially if you are offered stock options, profit sharing, pensions, insurance, and reimbursement accounts. Indeed, many individuals in the 1990s who took stock options in lieu of high salaries with start-up high tech firms discovered the importance of benefits when their benefits far outweighed their salaries; making only $30,000 a year, some of them became instant millionaires when their companies went public! In fact, the U.S. Department of Labor estimates that benefits now constitute 43 percent of total compensation for the average worker. For example, a $60,000 offer with Company X may translate into a compensation package worth $80,000; but a $50,000 offer with Company Y may actually be worth more than $100,000 when you examine their different benefits.

If the salary offered by the employer does not meet your expectations, but you still want the job, you might try to negotiate for some benefits which are not considered standard. These might include longer paid vacations, some flex-time, and profit sharing. Again, anything is "possible" if you know how to negotiate like a professional and you have a willing party who is eager to hire you.

Avoid Playing Unprofessional Games

If you get a job offer but you are considering other employers, let the others know you have a job offer. Telephone them to inquire about your status as well as inform them of the job offer. Sometimes this will prompt employers to make a hiring decision sooner than anticipated. In addition you will be informing them that you are in demand; they should seriously consider you before you get away!

Some job seekers play a bluffing game by telling employers they have alternative job offers even though they don't. Some candidates do this and get away with it. We don't recommend this approach. Not only is it dishonest, it will work to your disadvantage if the employer learns that you were lying. But more important, you should be selling yourself on the basis of your strengths rather than your deceit and greed. If you can't sell yourself honestly, don't expect to get along well on the job. When you compromise your integrity, you demean your value to others and yourself.

Take Time to Consider the Offer

You should accept an offer only after reaching a salary agreement. If you jump at an offer, you may appear needy. Take time to consider your options. Remember, you are committing your time and effort in exchange for money and status. Is this the job you really want? Take some time to think about the offer before giving the employer a definite answer. But don't play hard-to-get and thereby create ill will with your new employer.

While considering the offer, ask yourself several of the same questions you should have asked earlier on in your job search:

- What do I want to be doing five years from now?
- How will this job affect my personal life?
- Do I want to travel?
- Do I know enough about the employer and the future of this organization?
- How have previous occupants of this position fared? Why did they leave?
- Are there other job opportunities that better meet my goals?

Accepting a job is serious business. If you make a mistake, you could be locked into a very unhappy situation for a long time.

If you receive one job offer while considering another, you will be able to compare relative advantages and disadvantages. You also will have some external leverage for negotiating salary and benefits. While you should not play games, let the employer know you have alternative job offers. This communicates that you are in demand, others also know your value, and the employer's price is not the only one in town. Use this leverage to negotiate your salary, benefits, and job responsibilities.

Get the Job Offer in Writing

You should take notes throughout the salary negotiation session. Jot down pertinent information about the terms of employment. At the end of the session, before you get up to leave, **summarize** what you understand will be included in the compensation package and show it in outline form to the employer. Make sure both you and the employer understand the terms of employment, including specific elements in the compensation package.

If you accept the position, be sure to ask the employer to put the offer in writing, which may be in the form of a **letter of agreement**. This document should spell out your duties and responsibilities as well as detail how you will be compensated. If your agreement includes incentivized pay, make sure it details exactly how your commissions or bonuses will work – how and when they will be paid, set up, and measured. For example, will you be paid at the end of each quarter or at the end of the year? Do you receive a flat bonus, such as $1,000, or a percentage of the sales from an income stream.

Ask the employer to e-mail you a copy of this document for your review. Let him know you'll get back with him immediately. This document should serve as your employment contract.

13

Salaries for 900+ Occupations

"Most people are relatively 'salary dumb' – they know very little about what other people make. As a result, they are at a disadvantage when it comes time to negotiating salary and benefits. Salary knowledge is power!"

HOW MUCH CAN YOU EXPECT to make on the outside? Where can you get information on salaries for particular occupations and for specific communities? While you can find several nationwide and regional salary surveys in your local library and online, most are irrelevant to your particular local situation. Different communities, organizations, and employers can account for as much as 40 percent variation in average salaries. If in 2017 you planned to work in Cedar Rapids, Iowa as a **heavy and tractor-trailer truck driver** ($58,980 per year), you could expect to make 23 percent less than if you worked at the same job in San Francisco, California ($71,120 per year).

Take, for example, salaries for **dental assistants**. According to the U.S. Department of Labor's salary estimates for May 2016, the salary range for dental assistants was $25,460 to $52,000 a year, depending on the industry and location and whether the job was part-time or full-time. Dental assistants averaged the following annual salaries in these top paying metropolitan areas:

- Haverhill-Newburyport-Amesbury Town, MA-NH $50,140
- Minneapolis-St. Paul-Bloomington, MN-WI $48,430
- Nashua, NH-MA $47,940
- San Jose-Sunnyvale-Santa Clara, CA $47,840
- San Rafael, CA $47,840
- Santa Rosa, CA $47,090
- Rochester, MN $46,820
- Bridgeport-Stamford-Norwalk, CT $46,360
- Silver Spring-Frederick-Rockville, MD $46,360
- San Francisco-Redwood City-South San Francisco, CA $46,060

However, many metropolitan and nonmetropolitan areas in the South paid much less – $25,000-$36,000 a year.

The U.S. Department of Labor compiles an extensive database on over 900 occupations across the country. You can access this database by visiting the "Salary Finder" section of their CareerOneStop website:

www.careeronestop.org/explorecareers/plan/salaries.aspx

This is a great tool for researching most occupations by location. For example, if you're looking for salary information on **Landscaping and Groundskeeping Workers** in your favorite metropolitan area for 2017, just key in the occupation and city, and you'll get the following low to high salary range information:

Metro Area	Low/High Median Annual Salary
▪ **Nationwide**	**$19,160 - $41,070**
▪ Atlanta, GA	$19,320 - $39,390
▪ Baltimore, MD	$19,360 - $38,620
▪ Boston, MA	$23,010 - $48,390
▪ Chicago, IL	$19,950 - $46,360
▪ Cincinnati, OH	$18,550 - $38,410
▪ Cleveland, OH	$18,180 - $39,250
▪ Columbus, OH	$18,960 - $39,040
▪ Dallas, TX	$20,000 - $38,220
▪ Denver, CO	$20,540 - $41,860
▪ Detroit, MI	$19,320 - $43,580
▪ Houston, TX	$18,420 - $38,610
▪ Kansas City, MO	$20,210 - $39,960
▪ Las Vegas, NV	$17,880 - $42,070
▪ Los Angeles, CA	$21,160 - $52,410
▪ Miami, FL	$18,100 - $37,610
▪ Minneapolis, MN	$20,400 - $53,530
▪ Orlando, FL	$18,700 - $34,790
▪ Philadelphia, PA	$21,000 - $46,700
▪ Phoenix, AZ	$18,780 - $36,650
▪ Pittsburgh, PA	$18,120 - $42,510
▪ Portland, OR	$22,480 - $46,750
▪ Riverside, CA	$20,810 - $39,580
▪ Sacramento, CA	$21,550 - $44,980
▪ Saint Louis, MO	$20,550 - $39,070
▪ San Diego, CA	$20,820 - $46,210

- San Francisco, CA $22,260 - $70,190
- Seattle, WA $25,890 - $58,140
- Tampa, FL $18,860 - $35,020
- Washington, DC $20,700 - $44,250

You will discover salary ranges for all occupations will vary from one community to another. It's important to conduct your own local salary research rather than rely on highly generalized salary ranges from nationwide data which may be 2-4 years old.

According to *U.S. News & World Report*'s latest (2017) ranking, the 25 highest paying jobs in the U.S. for 2017 consist of the following:

Rank	Title	Median Annual Salary
1	Anesthesiologist	$187,200
2	Surgeon	$187,200
3	Oral and Maxillofacial Surgeon	$187,200
4	Obstetrician and Gynecologist	$187,200
5	Orthodontist	$187,200
6	Physician	$187,200
7	Psychiatrist	$187,200
8	Pediatrician	$170,300
9	Dentist	$152,700
10	Prosthodontist	$119,740
11	Nurse Anesthetist	$157,140
12	Petroleum Engineer	$129,990
13	IT Manager	$131,600
14	Marketing Manager	$128,750
15	Lawyer	$115,820
16	Podiatrist	$119,340
17	Financial Manager	$117,990
18	Sales Manager	$113,860
19	Business Operations Manager	$97,730
20	Pharmacists	$121,500
21	Financial Advisor	$89,160
22	Optometrist	$103,900
23	Mathematician	$111,110
24	Actuary	$97,070
25	Medical and Health Services Manager	$94,500

Most of these jobs require very high levels of education and training as well as are disproportionately found in the medical, business, and financial fields.

Similar and more detailed data can be obtained through the U.S. Department of Labor's OneStopCareer website (Salary Finder section again) and filtered by location (state) and education level. For example, the highest paying occupations in **California** for someone with a **high school diploma** or equivalent are the following:

Rank	Title	Median Annual Salary
25	First-Line Supervisors of Police and Detectives	$134,700
78	Electrical Power-Line Installers and Repairers	$104,200
86	Elevator Installers and Repairers	$100,000
98	Police and Sheriff's Patrol Officers	$98,200
103	Power Plant Operators	$96,700
115	First-Line Supervisors of Correctional Officers	$93,700
123	Detectives and Criminal Investigators	$92,500
128	Transportation, Storage, and Distribution Managers	$91,200
132	Gas Plant Operators	$89,900
142	Pile-Driver Operators	$87,000
150	Construction and Building Inspectors	$84,700
156	Gaming Managers	$83,200
159	Commercial Pilots	$82,100
164	Boilermakers	$81,600
171	Media and Communication Equipment Workers	$80,600
174	Rail Transportation Workers	$79,700
180	Power Distributors and Dispatchers	$79,300
186	Petroleum Pump System Operators, Refinery Operators, and Gaugers	$77,500
188	Stationary Engineers and Boiler Operators	$77,100
191	Postmasters and Mail Superintendents	$76,700

Ironically, some of the best paying occupations in California for individuals with a high school education are associated with the criminal justice and incarceration systems – police and correctional officers.

Index

Re-Entry Success Resources

THE FOLLOWING RE-ENTRY resources are available from Impact Publications. Full descriptions of each, as well as downloadable catalogs, video clips, and excerpts for many at www.impactpublications.com. Complete the following form or list the titles, include shipping (see formula at the end), enclose payment, and send your order to:

IMPACT PUBLICATIONS
7820 Sudley Road, Suite 100
Manassas, VA 20109
1-800-361-1055 (orders only)
Tel. 703-361 7300 or Fax 703-335-9486
Email: query@impactpublications.com
Quick & easy online ordering: www.impactpublications.com

Orders from individuals must be prepaid by check, money order, or major credit card. We accept telephone, fax, and email orders. Some titles are available on the GSA Schedule.

Qty.	TITLES	Price	TOTAL
Featured Title			
_____	The Ex-Offender's Job Interview Guide	$13.95	_____
Ex-Offender and Re-Entry Success Books			
_____	9 to 5 Beats Ten to Life	$20.00	_____
_____	99 Days and a Get Up	9.95	_____
_____	99 Days to Re-Entry Success Journal	4.95	_____
_____	Best Jobs for Ex-Offenders	11.95	_____
_____	Best Resumes and Letters for Ex-Offenders	19.95	_____
_____	Beyond Bars	14.95	_____
_____	Chicken Soup for the Prisoner's Soul	14.95	_____
_____	The Ex-Offender's 30/30 Job Solution	11.95	_____
_____	The Ex-Offender's Guide to a Responsible Life	15.95	_____
_____	The Ex-Offender's New Job Finding and Survival Guide	19.95	_____
_____	The Ex-Offender's Quick Job Hunting Guide	11.95	_____
_____	The Ex-Offender's Re-Entry Assistance Directory	29.95	_____
_____	The Ex-Offender's Re-Entry Success Guide	11.95	_____
_____	Finding a Job After Losing Your Way	14.00	_____
_____	Houses of Healing	15.00	_____
_____	How to Do Good After Prison	19.95	_____
_____	Jobs for Felons	7.95	_____
_____	Life Beyond Loss	20.00	_____
_____	Man, I Need a Job	7.95	_____
_____	Picking Up the Pieces	20.00	_____
_____	Quick Job Search for Ex-Offenders	7.95	_____
_____	Serving Productive Time	14.95	_____
_____	Support Programs for Ex-Offenders	40.00	_____
Ex-Offender Re-Entry DVDs			
_____	Construction Trade Options for Ex-Offenders (21 DVDs)	$2,149.00	_____
_____	Countdown to Freedom (6 DVDs)	695.00	_____
_____	Expert Job Search Strategies for Ex-Offenders (3 DVDs)	399.00	_____
_____	From Parole to Payroll (3 DVDs)	299.85	_____
_____	In Your Hands: Life After Prison	169.95	_____
_____	Preparing for Success: Ex-Offenders in Transition	$79.95	_____
_____	Putting the Bars Behind You	99.00	_____
_____	Resumes, Cover Letters, and Portfolios for Ex-Offenders	108.00	_____
_____	Road to Reentry Success Video Series (5 DVDs)	633.95	_____
_____	Starting Fresh With a Troubled Background (3 DVDs)	299.95	_____
_____	Stop Recidivism, Now! (3 DVDs)	275.00	_____

Prison Survival

_____	Map Through the Maze	11.95 _____
_____	The Now What? Project (2 DVDs)	199.95 _____
_____	Why Bother? (DVD)	119.95 _____

Independent Living & Managing Money

_____	21st Century Money Management DVD Series	$349.00 _____
_____	Are You Ready to Live on Your Own?	49.95 _____
_____	Buying the Basics (2 DVDs)	199.00 _____

Pocket Guides *(Contract #GS-02F-0146X)*

_____	Anger Management Pocket Guide	$2.95 _____
_____	Military Personal Finance Pocket Guide	2.95 _____
_____	Military Spouse's Employment Pocket Guide	2.95 _____
_____	Military-to-Civilian Transition Pocket Guide	2.95 _____
_____	Quick Job Finding Pocket Guide	3.95 _____
_____	Re-Entry Employment & Life Skills Pocket Guide	3.95 _____
_____	Re-Entry Personal Finance Pocket Guide	2.95 _____
_____	Re-Entry Start-Up Pocket Guide	2.95 _____
_____	Re-Imagining Life on the Outside Pocket Guide	3.95 _____

Finding Jobs and Getting Hired

_____	The 2-Hour Job Search	$12.99 _____
_____	Change Your Job, Change Your Life	21.95 _____
_____	Job Hunting Tips for People With Hot and Not-So-Hot Backgrounds	17.95 _____
_____	Knock 'Em Dead: The Ultimate Job Search Guide	17.99 _____
_____	No One Will Hire Me!	15.95 _____
_____	Overcoming Employment Barriers	19.95 _____
_____	Overcoming Barriers to Employment Success	18.95 _____
_____	The Quick 30/30 Job Solution	14.95 _____
_____	What Color is Your Parachute?	19.99 _____

Resumes and Cover Letters

_____	101 Best Resumes	$20.00 _____
_____	201 Dynamite Job Search Letters	19.95 _____
_____	Best KeyWords for Resumes, Cover Letters, and Interviews	19.95 _____
_____	Best Resumes for People Without a Four-Year Degree	19.95 _____
_____	High Impact Resumes and Letters	19.95 _____
_____	Knock 'Em Dead Cover Letters	14.99 _____
_____	Knock 'Em Dead Resumes	14.99 _____
_____	Military-to-Civilian Resumes and Letters	21.95 _____
_____	Modernize Your Job Search Letters	18.95 _____
_____	Modernize Your Resume	18.95 _____
_____	Resume, Application, and Letter Tips for People With Hot and Not-so-Hot Backgrounds	17.95 _____
_____	Resumes for Dummies	18.99 _____
_____	Salary Negotiation Tips for Professionals	16.95 _____
_____	Winning Letters That Overcome Barriers to Employment	17.95 _____

Interviewing and Salary Nagotiations

_____	101 Dynamite Questions to Ask At Your Job Interview	$13.95 _____
_____	101 Great Answers to the Toughest Interview Questions	12.99 _____
_____	Best Answers to 202 Job Interview Questions	17.95 _____
_____	Give Me More Money!	17.95 _____
_____	I Can't Believe They Asked Me That!	17.95 _____
_____	Job Interview Tips for People With Not-So-Hot Backgrounds	14.95 _____
_____	KeyWords to Nail Your Job Interview	17.95 _____
_____	Win the Interview, Win the Job	15.95 _____
_____	You Should Hire Me!	15.95 _____

Job Keeping and Revitalization

_____	How to Be a Star At Work	$15.00 _____

_____	The One Thing You Need to Know	29.95	_____
_____	Overcoming 101 More Employment Barriers	19.95	_____
_____	What Your Boss Doesn't Tell You Until It's Too Late	13.95	_____
_____	Who Gets Promoted, Who Doesn't, and Why	14.95	_____

Special Value Kits

_____	77 Re-Entry Success Books for Ex-Offenders	$1,220.95	_____
_____	Ace the Interview and Salary Negotiation Kit	472.95	_____
_____	Attitude, Purpose, and Passion Are Everything Kit	916.95	_____
_____	Discover What You're Best At Kit	450.95	_____
_____	Ex-Offender's Business Start-Up Kit	458.95	_____
_____	Faith-Based Re-Entry Solutions Kit	338.95	_____
_____	How to Be a Success at Work Kit	677.95	_____
_____	Job Finding With Social Media and Technology Kit	282.95	_____
_____	Learning From Successes and Failures Kit	1,019.95	_____
_____	Overcoming Barriers to Employment Kit	566.95	_____
_____	Overcoming Self-Defeating Behaviors and Bouncing Back Kit	247.95	_____
_____	The Ultimate Job Finding and Joyful Living Kit	379.95	_____

DVD Programs

_____	135 Interview Answers	$169.95	_____
_____	175 Resume Secrets	169.95	_____
_____	207 Interview Techniques	169.95	_____
_____	Common Job Interview Mistakes	99.95	_____
_____	Digital Communication Skills	129.95	_____
_____	Dress and Groom for Career Success	156.95	_____
_____	E-Networking for Jobs	129.95	_____
_____	Get Hired and Go	599.95	_____
_____	Getting the Job You Really Want	995.00	_____
_____	Good First Impressions	156.95	_____
_____	Job Seeker: Interview Do's and Don'ts	169.95	_____
_____	Navigating the World of Social Media	108.00	_____
_____	Soft Skills in the Workplace	156.95	_____
_____	What Will I Say at the Interview?	129.95	_____
_____	You're Fired!	156.95	_____

SUBTOTAL _____

TERMS: Individuals must prepay; approved accounts are billed net 30 days. All orders under $100.00 should be prepaid.

RUSH ORDERS: fax, call, or email for more information on any special shipping arrangements and charges.

Virginia residents add 6% sales tax _____
California residents add ___% sales tax _____

Shipping ($5 +8% of SUBTOTAL) _____
TOTAL ORDER _____

Bill To:

Name_____	Title _____
Address _____	
City _____	State/Zip _____
Phone ( )_____	(daytime)
Email _____	

Ship To: (if different from "Bill To;" include street delivery address) :

Name_____	Title _____
Address _____	
City _____	State/Zip _____
Phone ( )_____	(daytime)
Email _____	

PAYMENT METHOD:

❑ **Purchase Order** #_____ *(attach or fax with this order form)*

❑ **Check** – Make payable to IMPACT PUBLICATIONS

❑ **Credit Card**: ❑ Visa ❑ MasterCard ❑ AMEX ❑ Discover

Card #													Expiration Date		

	Name on Card (print)	